AF241203

PAI-CHIA CH'ÜAN
(PAI FAMILY FIST)

Dedication

This manual is dedicated to Jackie, Chris, and Julie!

Since Jackie and I have known each other,

and for our kids' entire lives,

they have put up with and given their time and effort,

directly and indirectly,

to my obsession with martial arts.

An unrepayable debt!

This publication would not have been possible without them!

PAI-CHIA CH'ÜAN
(PAI FAMILY FIST)

Pai-Lum Kung-Fu

as taught by the

Pai Family Martial Training Association
Volume 1

General Information • History • Theory • Fundamentals

by

William Luciano

DISCLAIMER

Please note that the author and publisher of this manual are NOT RESPONSIBLE in any manner whatsoever for any injury that may result from practicing the techniques or following any instructions given within. Since the physical activities described herein may be too strenuous for some readers to engage in safely, a physician must be consulted before training.

COPYRIGHT © 2026 • ALL RIGHTS RESERVED
WILLIAM LUCIANO
PIERIAN SPRINGS PRESS

FIRST EDITION, May 2026
ISBN 978-1-965784-32-7 PAPERBACK
Printed in the United States of America, Canada, Australia, Saudi Arabia, Japan, India, Brazil, and the European Union.

Cover Design & Book Typography by **William Luciano**
Typefaces licensed Adobe, Linotype, Emigre, & URW GmbH.

PierianSpringsPress.Com
PIERIAN SPRINGS PRESS, INC
30 N GOULD ST, STE 25398
SHERIDAN, WYOMING 82801-6317

TABLE OF CONTENTS

Chinese Terminology used in this manual

The Chinese terminology used in this manual is primarily from the Mandarin dialect. Other dialects, such as Cantonese or Hokkien, may also be used if it is a more recognizable or popular version of a word or phrase. In some instances, Japanese, Hawaiian, or Okinawan terms are used.

This publication uses two systems of romanization of the Mandarin dialect: Wade-Giles, and Pinyin.

Wade-Giles is the oldest method of romanization used; our preferred system for proper names, martial art systems, form sequences, historical names, geographical locations, and key phrases.

Pinyin has become the new standard system of romanization adopted by mainland China. Most people in the world use the pinyin system of romanization. Eventually, we will switch to this method.

Romanization and language key:

Wade-Giles [WG]   Hokkien [HOK]

Pinyin [PY]   Okinawan [OK]

Cantonese [CAN]   Japanese [JAP]

If there is no superscript key following a Chinese word, it will be from the Wade-Giles romanization system.

I have spent most of my life associated with martial arts; many of the people I consider friends I have met through martial arts.

Daniel K. Pai and six distinct groups of people have contributed significantly to my understanding of the Pai Family Art. Including the application, history of this art, being part of a martial tradition, and what it was like to train with Daniel K. Pai. These groups are:

Daniel K. Pai: The founder and primary source of knowledge for everyone that trains Pai-Lum.

My primary teachers: David L. Smith, Marcia L. Pickands, and Rich Macey.

Students of Daniel K. Pai with whom I have trained (in seminars, classes, or private lessons): I have many hours of training with the first two people on this list: Thomas D. St. Charles, Phil Hunter, John Weninger, Steve Mathews, Robert Skaling, Thomas Sanders, Patrick McCarthy, Robert Dutcher, George Chartier, Martin Pickands, and Paul Olson.

Students of Daniel K. Pai, with whom I have not trained but have helped immensely with information about Grandmaster Pai, Pai-Lum history, and insight: David Everett, Karen Tolczyk, Russell Hudson, Charles Powell, Fred Schmitz, Ron Lydestad, Bruce Currie, Ken Tallack, Rick Hodish, Terry Cermola, Tony Carpanzano, Thomas Wolfinger, Bill Rolfe, Mike Kaylor, Clarence Cooper, Honey Silk, Shawn Dick, John Riddick, Laurie Ring, Bruce McKnight, Al Mueller, George Dillman, Warren Cottrell, and Hampton Finney.

Kung-Fu brothers, sisters, cousins, and students: The many people that I have trained with and the people that I have taught the art to.

People who were not students of Daniel Pai but knew of him, helped me find information, and inspired me to go deeper in both my training and research: Steven Nacua, Patrick Hodges, and Bruce Juchnik. Mr. Nacua also shared his personal experiences of what it was like to grow up and train martial arts in the plantations of Hawai'i.

Archivists and Researchers: These individuals were very generous in sharing their research, documents, and personal archives: Marcia Pickands, Martin Pickands, David L. Smith, Russell Hudson, Patrick McCarthy, Zhuang Jiaren [莊嘉仁], Stephen Maddux, Ken Tallack, Carmen Spagnola, and Milton Rivera.

In addition, the individuals that have helped with the nuts and bolts part of putting a manuscript together: Martin Pickands, Patrick McCarthy, Phil Hunter, Terry Cermola, Norman Johnson, and Russell Hudson.

Photo Credits

The photos in this manual were initially taken by or come from the collections of the following people:

Photographers: David Everett, Gary LaVallee, Christopher Lee Helton, Peter Stoddard, Martin Pickands, James Wilson, Charles Powell, Ray Carpenter, William Luciano.

From the collections of: David L. Smith, Marcia & Martin Pickands, John Weninger, George Dillman, Puelai Pai, and William Luciano.

Joshua Tweed, Shane Diel, and Edward Sean Buckley are the practitioners demonstrating techniques in chapter seven.

If there are any errors in crediting the photos in this manuscript, contact me; it will be corrected in future editions.

The information in this document is a product of my training, research, and understanding of the principles, martial theory, fundamentals, form sequences, usage, and history of the Pai Family Arts.

The primary goal of this manual is to provide basic information about Chinese martial arts in general and Pai-Chia Ch'üan (Pai-Lum Kung-Fu) in particular for students and practitioners of this art. History, martial arts definitions, principles, theory, fundamentals, form sequences, and introductory applications are covered.

The idea for this publication began in 1990 when I began to work on a school manual for my training hall, the White Dragon Kung-Fu Center, in Albany, NY. I wanted to create a document or manual to educate new students and provide an accurate resource for practitioners to understand these arts better.

In developing this manual, I have taken great pains to ensure accurate information about our art, martial arts in general, people, and events related to Daniel K. Pai's teachings. Like most martial arts, our early history is full of conjecture. It was challenging to find information on this system that was not incorrect, incomplete, or purposely manipulated to fit or validate particular individuals' specific needs or points of view, including some who had never trained in Pai-Lum. It did not help my cause that Grandmaster Pai did not entirely trust anyone, including his closest and most senior students. He often told them contradicting stories about our history (e.g., teachers with whom he trained, where some of our curricula came from, names of techniques, and form sequences). At times, it seemed like Grandmaster Pai purposely drove wedges between some of his students, keeping them at odds.

I had access to my teacher's libraries, including notes, notebooks, internal documents, letters, handouts, videos, and manuals issued by the Pai-Lum Association, Grandmaster Pai's White Lotus Society, the Pai-Shou Athletic Association, and various training halls associated with these organizations. There were many personal letters and internal communications between Grandmaster Pai and his students; I found some of them to have interesting and educational information. None were meant for public viewing; they were not used in this publication.

There was good information in some of the notes (mostly class notes taken by Marcia Pickands in the seventies, and a multitude from David L. Smith that date from the early seventies to May of two thousand twenty-three) and notebooks (from David L. Smith and Marcia Pickands). I found very little information in most of the handouts and manuals. Many were lists of criteria for the different skills, self-defense applications, form sequences, and grading requirements for different periods. There was not much in the context of explanation, accurate history, or representation of what most Pai-Lum training halls taught. My teachers (who had been tasked to put many of these manuals together) shared this observation.

The documents I found most consistent with what I was looking to do were the *Pai-Lum policy document 1980-001* and Dave Everett's *White Lotus Kung-Fu Center Student Manual* from the early eighties. I roughly based the original layout and content on these documents.

I have decided not to include an in-depth history of martial arts. Many books, translations, papers, and magazines have covered that topic far more accurately than I could. Instead, I have included some general information about Chinese martial arts and how they relate to our art. This publication will record our history, origin, martial content, and training theories.

My hope is that this manual can be a resource for every Pai-Lum practitioner: a truthful, documented history of how the art developed from the mid-nineteen-sixties until now.

William Luciano,

September 18, 2024

Pai-Chia Ch'üan (Pai-Lum)

Pai-Lin Ch'üan

Shaolin Shi-Pa T'eng-Jen Fa

Foreword

BY

Patrick McCarthy

Patrick McCarthy

It is with deep respect and genuine admiration that I offer this foreword for William Luciano's comprehensive exploration of Pai Family Kung Fu. Having been associated with the Pai Family Arts since 1973, I can attest to the depth, richness, and unique cultural heritage that this martial tradition embodies.

This book is not just a manual; it is a testament to the enduring legacy of Grandmaster Daniel K. Pai and the generations of practitioners who have dedicated their lives to preserving and evolving this art. William Luciano has done a remarkable job in distilling decades of knowledge, experience, and tradition into a resource that is both informative and inspirational. His dedication to accuracy and his deep understanding of the Pai Family system shine through on every page. For those new to Pai-Lum or martial arts in general, this book provides a solid foundation and a window into the profound world of Chinese martial arts. For seasoned practitioners, it offers a detailed guide that reinforces the core principles and advanced concepts of the art.

Patrick McCarthy with Grandmaster Daniel K. Pai in 1973

- Photo from the collection of Patrick McCarthy

I have had the privilege of knowing Bill Shifu for many years, and I have always been impressed by his remarkable physical and technical prowess, humility, open-minded approach to learning, and unwavering commitment to the art. His passion for martial arts and his desire to educate others are evident in his teaching and in the pages of this book. His ability to articulate the nuances of Pai-Lum, while maintaining the integrity of its tradition, is a rare gift, and it will benefit anyone who reads this work.

XV

In writing this book, William Luciano has not only honored the memory and teachings of Grandmaster Pai, but he has also provided a valuable tool for future generations of martial artists. His work ensures that the Pai Family Arts will continue to thrive and evolve, staying relevant in a modern world while remaining deeply rooted in tradition.

I highly recommend this book to anyone who seeks to deepen their understanding of martial arts, whether you are a beginner or an advanced practitioner. May it serve as a guide, a reference, and a source of inspiration on your martial journey.

Patrick McCarthy

Founder,

International Ryukyu

Karate Research Society

William Luciano and Patrick McCarthy, Hanshi
Clifton Park, NY, 2015

FOREWORD

BY

STEVEN NACUA

Immigration to the territory of Hawai'i was at its height between 1920 and the late 1940s. People came from East Asia and parts of Europe. Many came to escape war and the hardship of life; they searched for a better life for themselves and their families. Hawai'i became a melting pot of mixed customs and cultures.

Steven Nacua

Those who came settled in Hawai'i, Maui, Lana'i, Moloka'i, O'ahu, and Kaua'i islands. Lifestyles for most that came, regardless of the island they chose to settle on, were almost identical. Sugar and Pineapples were the primary source of employment for many of the new arrivals. The companies built subdivisions called camps by the locals to house those they employed. Housing was not segregated by nationality or economic status, except for the Lunas (Overseers). The Lunas were housed away from the general population. Residents in the camp were of mixed nationalities and resided side by side with each other. Unintended by the companies, the mixing of nationalities was instrumental in introducing the residents to each other and helping them learn to understand and respect other cultures and customs.

The camp residents lived in harmony for generations. The geographical location of some camps was identified by the primary nationality that populated them. The Camps had Chinese, Spanish, Filipino, Japanese, or Korean identities. The locals did not consider it derogatory; it gave the people basic directions. For those of us who had an interest in learning martial arts, this was great. We knew where the masters lived and where they taught their arts.

Growing up in the camp taught us to appreciate, learn and share other customs and cultures. We celebrated festivals and holidays of all cultures. Integration of customs and cultures made it possible for the locals to co-exist without discrimination and help each other to co-exist in harmony. Most camp residents worked together in the sugar or pineapple fields or factories and became friends. Working side by side in the fields and factories brought people together and helped build trust and friendships. This trust and friendship helped to bridge the gap between customs and open doors to outsiders who were once considered just acquaintances.

A few who came during the first and second waves of migration were martial artists. Each martial artist brought the martial art learned in their respective countries. Many, if not all, who were known to be martial artists were highly skilled in their respective art. Some instructors were prohibited from teaching their art outside their family or nationality. The exception was Japanese martial arts.

Japanese martial arts were easier to access; anyone willing to learn was accepted. Other styles were more selective about whom they taught. To learn from these private groups, an individual had to be a family member or trusted by the instructor.

During the post-war era, martial arts became popular in Hawai‘i. Styles like Kajukenbo, Pai-Lum, Lima, and some less popular styles emerged onto the local scene. Although the Japanese and newer styles mentioned were open to the masses, some remained private and closed to outsiders. Martial arts founded in Hawai‘i during that post-war era were eclectic styles. Both Kajukenbo and Pai-Lum were at the forefront. In its infancy, Kajukenbo, the style taught by co-founders Adriano and Joseph Emperado, was mainly taught in Hawai‘i and eventually made it to the west coast.

In contrast, Pai Lum, the style developed by Daniel Pai, was mainly promoted in the continental US. These styles have flourished and have had a significant impact on the Martial Arts community. Highly reputable teachers and their students from the Kajukenbo and Pai-Lum systems continue to teach and perpetuate the teaching and method of their predecessors.

Daniel Pai, the founder of Mr. Luciano's style, Pai-Lum, is known for his reputation as a martial artist and an honored ambassador of martial arts. After his discharge from the military, Daniel Pai founded the Pai-Lum System. Techniques taught to Daniel Pai by his grandfather are deeply rooted in the Pai-Lum System. A branch of the Pai Lum system was inherited by Pai Ching Lin (AKA-David Smith) and is now perpetuated by instructors like William (Bill) Luciano.

I met William Luciano in 1987 when he was a student of Mrs. Marcia Pickands and Mr. David Smith at their Mo-Kwoon in Albany, New York, after relocating from Maui, Hawai‘i, to Glens Falls, New York. We've known each other and have been friends and fellow martial artists since then. We both have a strong interest in martial arts and a desire to help preserve Chinese Martial Arts. Mr. Luciano has achieved a high level of Skill and Proficiency in Chinese Martial Arts; he has trained in and teaches both Internal and External methods. Mr. Luciano has a vast knowledge of martial arts history and is skilled in theory and fundamental martial techniques. He is humble and open-minded and continues to improve his art and teach his system. He continues to learn and educate students and instructors by offering classes and seminars in the area and abroad. To hijack a saying from a mutual friend Dr. Alan Wong, William Luciano, and his school are "Gems of Martial Arts."

I highly recommend this book to beginners and advanced practitioners. Also, those wanting to gain insight into the history of Pai-Lum and an understanding of theory and fundamentals in Chinese Martial Arts. The uniqueness of his book is William Luciano's detailed instructions and understanding of martial arts.

I believe that to improve skill and proficiency in their art, one must recognize the weaknesses and strengths of their method and have an open mind without judgment or prejudice toward art. In conclusion, I believe that the ESSENCE of martial arts is inclusive in all styles and methods. This book is a valuable tool to have on your desk or in your library.

Steven Nacua

Hop Gar Pai, Pak Hok Pai,

Choy Li Fut, T'ai-Chi Ch'uan,

Kajukenbo Ch'uan-Fa Gung-Fu

Villabrille System of Kali

Mirafuentes Balintawak Eskrima

Steven Nacua, Sifu and William Luciano
Albany, NY 1991

INTRODUCTION

This manual is not about Daniel K. Pai per se but about a branch school of Pai-Lum developed primarily from his teachings. Documenting his life, accomplishments, experiences, and students in detail would take a substantial volume. However, to tell this story, it is essential to explain a little bit about his life, martial training, history, and the development of Pai-Lum Kung-Fu as we know it today!

Daniel K. Pai

白天龍

Pai T'ien-Lung

- From the collection of
George Dillman

Today, over thirty years after the passing of Grandmaster Daniel K. Pai, there are multiple branches or schools of Pai-Lum. These Schools are headed by Grandmaster Pai's senior (second-generation) students or their third-generation successors. Each school is based on these individual's experience, understanding, and interpretation of martial arts. Many of them had significant martial training before becoming students of Grandmaster Pai; others began their training in Pai-Lum. As a result, all of the existing schools teach slightly different methods. This manual represents David L. Smith's and Marcia Pickands' schools or branches of Pai-Lum Kung-Fu as taught by William Luciano.

> *"If a person seeks something true, he will want to understand the history, the philosophy and the tradition as to how it began. The problem is, many Americans don't have the patience."* - Daniel K. Pai

Our viewpoint of history in this manual is based on the information we have and the conjecture based on this information. We connect the dots of information we have and fill in the blanks with what we know about the martial arts culture of Hawai'i, histories of other Hawaiian-based arts, family genealogy, Daniel Pai's life events, military records, newspaper articles and advertisements, the US census, and stories from Daniel K. Pai, and his students.

This history may differ from or contradict much of what has been written about this subject.

Who is Daniel K. Pai?

In his lifetime, Daniel K. Pai was a cowboy, corpsman, husband, father, stuntman, actor, entertainer, bodyguard, healer, professor, minister, philosopher, and highly sought-after martial arts teacher! Between his military duties in the late fifties, work in the movie industry, martial training halls, concert security, personal protection, demonstrations, and people seeking him out for his martial expertise, his students, including several celebrities, numbered in the thousands during his lifetime.

An exceptional martial artist, Daniel K. Pai was a knowledgeable and powerful individual. His training was diverse, learning elements of several martial disciplines under many instructors. He claimed his primary training was in a Chinese-based family system under his grandfather. In addition, He had significant training in Judo, Jujutsu, Kempo, Karate, and Kenjutsu. As a teacher, he was insightful and demanding, a taskmaster who often pushed people further than they thought capable. He was a healer, having repaired or nursed back to health many students injured in their training.

Daniel K. Pai: A Timeline from 1930 to 1993

Daniel K. Pai's Mother, Mary K. Pa'i (born Mary Ku'uleialohapoinale Ma'ina'aupo), and her family spent much of her life growing up and living at the Parker Ranch in Hawai'i. His father, Joseph Pa'i, and his uncle, Samuel Ma'ina'aupo, AKA Sam Po, were famous cowboys; they also worked together at the Parker Ranch. It is assumed that Joseph Pa'i and Mary Ma'ina'aupo met through this connection.

Daniel Kane Pai (Born: Daniel Kalima'ahae Pa'i), the last of six children born to Mary and Joseph Pa'i, was born on the island of O'ahu, Hawai'i, on April 4, 1930. His family lived at the Kane'ohe Ranch, where his father was employed. After Joseph Pa'i passed away (May 1931), his family moved to Honolulu, where he lived until nineteen forty-six.

From age 5 to 16, he trained martial skills with family members, various instructors associated with Henry Okazaki, and possibly members of the Chinese community.

Daniel Pai, on his initial training in martial arts:

"I started playing around with it when I was five. I can't say that I really learned it then because, at that age, nobody really knows what he is doing. But I was around it and absorbing it .... I began to adapt to a form within a style by the time I was nine or ten. When other kids went out and played football or baseball, I went home to practice Kung-Fu."

At age sixteen, Daniel moved to the "Big Island" (the term Hawaiians use when talking about the island of Hawai'i), where he worked as a cowboy at the Parker Ranch for four years (1946 to 1950). On horseback, he herded and rounded up stray cattle, branded cattle, and trained wild horses for saddle riding. His name is mentioned in the book *Loyal to the Land: The Legendary Parker Ranch, 1950-1970, Volume 2*, as one of the younger ranch hands who was good with training horses. Like the plantations of Hawai'i, the Parker Ranch was a place of ethnic diversity where people from different cultures lived, worked, and trained together.

During his time at the ranch, he engaged in martial training with his uncles (Percy Kaliko Ma'ina'aupo, Sam Ma'ina'aupo, David Kawika Kauwe) and others. He continued his Jujutsu and Judo training with Himeo Fujitani at the Kohala Judo Club. On several occasions in the nineteen seventies, Daniel Pai had stated that he trained Kempo on the Big Island.

On July 21-22, 1950, Daniel Pai returned to O'ahu for an inter-island Jujutsu tournament between the Kohala Judo Club, Himeo Fujitani instructor, and the Aiea Judo Club, Richard Takamoto instructor. Daniel Pai and Eddie Coney were voted outstanding competitors in the team matches on the 22nd.

INTERISLE JUDO TOURNEY DRAWS CAPACITY HOUSE

Special Star-Bulletin Correspondence

WAIPAHU, July 24—A capacity house at the Aiea gym on both Friday and Saturday nights saw Kohala and the Aiea judo teams clash in an interisland jujitsu tourney.

Kohala beat Aiea, 7 to 6, in team match on Friday night with Dan Pai of Kohala and Eddie Coney of Aiea voted the two outstanding performances of the evening. They were presented trophies donated by Himeo Fujitani.

The two night interisland judo series was a complete success and the Aiea club and its instructor, Richard Takamoto, expresses its sincere thanks to the entire community for its interest and support.

- Honolulu Star Bullitin (Honolulu Hawai'i)
July 24, 1950

Cpl Danny K. Pai, 7071st Med Co, ASU, who does a novel Hawaiian song-and-dance act, including a short Hula routine, won "on a bye" to proceed to the MDW contest.

*- From the collection of
Puelai Pai*

At some point in the latter half of 1950, Daniel was again living in Honolulu, where he would stay until enlisting in the US Army.

On September 18, 1951, Daniel Pai enlisted in the US Army and became a corpsman attached to the 7071st SU (USAH) MED CO until September 24, 1953; he was actively deployed in Korea from February 1952 to December 1952. He re-enlisted for three years in the US Army Reserve from September 24, 1953, to September 24, 1956. An interesting note is that in his DA 20 (Enlisted Qualification Record, 9/11/1951), he listed basketball, boxing, and judo as hobbies and sports.

Daniel Pai was stationed in Korea, Japan, Washington DC, and Virginia from the early nineteen fifties. Except for a handful of finite dates, it is difficult to pinpoint where he was and when from December 1952 until the early nineteen sixties.

He was in Japan in September 1953 and, at some point in 1955, when he worked in the movie production "*The House of Bamboo.*" These time frames probably coincide with his training in Japan, Okinawa, and possibly Hong Kong. In the early nineteen seventies, he told David L. Smith that he trained with Gogen Yamaguchi (Goju-Ryu) and Morihei Ueshiba (Aikido) when he was stationed in Japan. He is also thought to have trained with Shigeru Nakamura (Okinawa Kenpo). Daniel Pai had some interaction with Shorin-Ji Kempo practitioners as well. (During the 1989 international Kuo-Shu tournament held in Las Vegas, NA, he introduced John Weninger to a gentleman named Gakuryo Reiun, a Shorin Ji Kempo practitioner, as "*...the only man I bow to...*").

In December 1955, Daniel was stationed at Fort Belvoir, Fairfax, Virginia; he lived in Alexandria, where he worked as a hairstylist and taught martial arts in addition to his military duties. He and his wife, Betsey, had two children: a son, Daniel Kalai Pai (1956), and a daughter, Puelai Mui Pai (1960). There is Newspaper verification that he was still living in Alexandria in June 1960. One of Daniel Pai's first training halls was on Mount Vernon Avenue in Alexandria, VA.

During his time in Virginia, he also worked for US Senator Hiram Fong, whom he called his "Uncle" when Senator Fong was in Washington, DC.

Between 1960 and late 1962, Daniel Pai was in Hawai'i working as a stuntman and extra in the movie industry. He worked in some episodes of "Hawaiian Eye," where he met Robert Conrad. In April of 1961, Daniel Pai was in Hawai'i (Kaua'i) working as a stuntman in the movie *"Blue Hawaii"* starring Elvis Presley. He was in Hawai'i when his mother passed away on July 13, 1961.

1962 again found Daniel K. Pai working in the film industry; he spent some time in Hawai'i and California as a stuntman and an extra in the movie *"Girls, Girls, Girls"* starring Elvis Presley. It was filmed on location in Honolulu and the Big Island of Hawai'i starting April 9, and the bulk of the filming in California starting May 1. On May 14, 1962, Daniel was honorably discharged from the Army Reserve.

In his book *"Prometheus: The George Dillman Story,"* George Dillman states that Ed Parker, a friend of Daniel K. Pai's from Hawai'i, invited Daniel to teach at his studios in California; this is somewhat corroborated by Robert Schoolnick, who said he met Daniel K. Pai in California in 1963 at one of Ed Parker's Martial Art Studios. (Mr. Schoolnick, who was eight years old then, would later train at the Fire Dragon school in Hartford in the nineteen seventies). Mr. Dillman also states that Ed Parker and Daniel Pai trained together in Hawai'i under William Chow; this could have happened when Daniel was between Military deployments in the nineteen fifties and early sixties.

Daniel K. Pai returned to Virginia in 1963. In 1966, he lived in Richmond, where he and Charles Armstrong were co-owners of the Richmond Judo and Karate Club on Broad Street. At this point, he was gaining a name for himself in the American martial arts scene. Attending, competing in, refereeing, and promoting tournaments throughout the eastern half of the United States. By 1968, he moved his training hall to West Broad Street, under a new name, Pai Defensive Art Studio.

Daniel Pai lived in Virginia until 1970, in Connecticut from 1970 to 1976, and in Florida from 1976 until his passing in 1993.

Daniel K. Pai's Martial History

We know little about Daniel K. Pai's martial background before nineteen sixty-five. We believe he had training in multiple arts, including Chinese methods. Undoubtedly, he must have had access to great teachers. The problem is that we do not know who they were; there was always a level of secrecy regarding this topic. Aside from talking about his grandfather, Daniel K. Pai did not openly discuss, in detail, who he trained with (many martial artists did not publicly share this knowledge). Some of his students believe he was told not to say who his teachers were. This statement is based on conversations with David L. Smith, Marcia Pickands, and Thomas St. Charles and the fact that no one I have talked to has been definitively able to answer this question.

In the following paragraphs, we will cover the state of Asian Martial Arts in Hawai'i when Daniel K. Pai began training, obstacles he would have had to overcome to train in the Chinese arts, his Chinese heritage, and Pai Po-Fong.

Asian Martial Arts in Hawai'i

Asian Martial Arts in Hawai'i during the early part of the twentieth century were as diverse as the people that lived there. There were methods from China, Japan, Okinawa, Korea, and the Philippines. Some were easily accessible, and others were shrouded in secrecy.

Since the nineteen twenties, thanks partly to Henry Okazaki, Japanese arts such as Jujutsu and Judo have been accessible and publicly taught to non-Japanese. Kempo, as taught by James Mitose and William K. S. Chow, has been publicly accessible since the nineteen forties. Almost every YMCA or social club offered some sport or self-defense-based classes on Jujutsu, Wrestling, Judo, Kempo, Karate, or Boxing. Daniel K. Pai's introduction to these arts may have come from similar sources.

Chinese martial arts, collectively known as Chinese Boxing, were generally not accessible to everyone; one had to be Chinese, a family member, and a trusted individual; there were very few exceptions. As a rule, Chinese social organizations[1] (where martial arts are generally taught) did not always allow people of mixed ethnic backgrounds to train in martial arts. By the nineteen thirties, some of these organizations did have members of Chinese-Hawaiian ancestry.

---

1 At this point in history, most of the Chinese benevolent associations and the Chinese population in Hawai'i were located in, or near, the Chinatown area of O'ahu.

Obstacles: Culture, Language, and Age

When Daniel K. Pai began his martial training, the arts were still primarily taught to people from the same ethnic background from which a particular art originated. He would have had several obstacles deterring him from learning Chinese martial arts; the most obvious was being of Hawaiian-Chinese heritage. Another is that he was raised in a Hawaiian culture, not Chinese; he had stated on multiple occasions that the Hawaiians and the Chinese did not entirely accept him.

"... because of the blood-lines that my ancestors came from, I was not allowed to train in certain schools..." - Daniel K. Pai

Language would also have been a barrier; Daniel Pai grew up in a world that used many languages. Hawaiian Pidgin English had become the primary language most of Hawaii's population used. He was exposed to English, Hawaiian, Pidgin English, Japanese, and Chinese (primarily Chung-Shan Cantonese). He was fluent in English, Hawaiian, Pidgin English, and Japanese (this may have happened when he was stationed in Japan during the nineteen fifties). He had a working knowledge of, but was not fluent in, Chinese; his knowledge, understanding, and usage were probably from interacting with family members, Chinese individuals, and Pidgin English. Age would have been another barrier.

Daniel K. Pai's Chinese Heritage

Daniel K. Pai's Chinese heritage comes from the maternal side of his family. His maternal grandparents were Joseph Kalipo "Po" Maʻinaʻaupo (1854-1935), who was Hawaiian, and Harriet "Hattie" Maʻinaʻaupo (1861-1928), who was half Chinese and half Caucasian. Harriet Maʻinaʻaupo's maiden name was listed as Ing[2] [In, Ying, Jin 然]; her parents are listed as Mr. Ah Ing [Ahin, Ahjin, 阿然] and Anne Ing (maiden name Nowlien). Ah Ing probably had some martial training; self-defense experience would have been prudent. We speculate that if this were the case, then elements of the art would have been taught to Daniel Pai's grandmother, mother, uncles, aunts, and older brother Joseph by his great-grandfather. This would be the source if Daniel Pai's Chi-

---

2 Ing may not be a surname. Chinese names usually have three characters, the first being the surname and the other two combining for the given name; this often leads to confusion because the surname is last in English and Hawaiian. Some Chinese people in Hawaiʻi use just one character from their given names, leading to the prefix Ah [阿] being added to the single character ie. Ah In, or Ah Fong.

nese martial training comes from his biological family. Daniel Pai never met his great-grandfather or grandmother, as they had passed away before he was born. He would have to have learned elements of this art from his uncles, aunts, and older brother Joseph (1913-1978).

Daniel Pai did know his maternal grandfather and may have learned rudimentary elements of the Hawaiian arts from him. Joseph Ma'ina'aupo passed away in 1935 when Daniel Pai was 4 or 5.

Daniel Pai's stepfather, Herman Kane (Herman Halemano Kane 1906-1948), is listed in the US census as Chinese-Hawaiian; this may have also opened some doors for Daniel's training in the Chinese arts.

Herman was involved with Mary Pai since the mid-1930s; they married in December 1942. Herman Kane must have been somewhat influential in Daniel Pai's life; Daniel used Kane as his middle name after moving to the mainland US.

This ancestry and having someone in good standing vouch for him may have opened some doors, allowing him access to instruction in the Chinese arts.

In an article by John T. McGee, *Danny Pai, The Controversial Powerhouse*, published in the July 1973 issue of Official Karate Magazine, Daniel Pai states that his grandmother brought him to a Chinese school to learn how to kick and defend himself (in the mid-nineteen thirties). During his first class, his grandfather came in, and everyone bowed to him; at this point, Daniel Pai realized his grandfather was a master (of martial arts).

Daniel K. Pai's Grandfather

Daniel K. Pai credited much of his training to his grandfather, who, over the years, has been referred to by multiple names, including Chuan, Po, Po Fong, and Pai Po-Fong. The following is an excerpt from a letter written by David L. Smith in April 1974:

> *"... His martial art was taught to him by his grandfather. Master Pai is not given to speaking in detail about his past, saying only that his grandfather was a "merchant" in the islands and his name was often pronounced, "Po..."*

Once, when asked about his grandfather, Daniel Pai answered, "He was a merchant." In response to additional questions about his grandfather, he leaned forward and, in an ominously authoritative manner, responded, "He was a merchant," implying he was an important, private, and influential individual, then changed the subject!

Pai Po-Fong

Since the mid-seventies, Daniel K. Pai's grandfather has been referred to as Pai Po-Fong by all practitioners of Pai-Lum; many stories and training methods are attributed to him. In the early seventies, the name Pai Po-Fong was found in a manuscript on Mushindo-Ryu Karate compiled by Terrance Dukes in 1971. Pai Po Fong appears twice in the manuscript, once, on page twenty, listed as one of the past masters whose names were recited at a White Lotus Temple; the other (spelled Pai Pou Fong) is included in a martial arts lineage on page twenty-three. Some people believed this to be Daniel K. Pai's grandfather. However, the list of past masters and the lineage chart clearly indicate that these two spellings were incorrect romanizations of Pai Yue-Feng [白玉峰 Pak Yook-Fong [CAN]], a famous historical figure of Shaolin fame, who lived in the mid-1500s, not Pai Po-Fong, the merchant, who would have lived in Hawai'i in the early part of the 20th century.

Summation

On the subject of Pai Po-Fong, there is no simple or accurate answer as to who he was. On the one hand, we know that he could not be a biological grandfather to Daniel Pai; his grandfathers passed away in 1935. Nor does he appear to have been a relative of Herman Kane, Daniel Pai's stepfather. On the other hand, Daniel Pai talked about him often with such emotion that it would lead us to believe that Pai Po-Fong was real; this could be possible if his grandfather were a martial relation.

While there is a chance that a person named Pai Po-Fong existed, there is no record we can find of anyone with that name[3]. We believe that Pai Po-Fong is a compound name metaphorically representing all of Daniel Pai's influential teachers, allowing him to talk about his teacher(s) and maintain secrecy about his training.

------

3 It is not unusual in Chinese culture for people to have up to five different names in their lifetime; they are Birth name [Ch'iu Ming 取名], Formal or Personal name [Ta Ming 大名], Assumed name [Hao 號], Courtesy or Style name [Tzu 字], and Pen name [Pi Ming 筆名 or Pi Hao 筆號]. In addition, some Chinese people in Hawai'i have been known to use hybrid names that combine Chinese and Hawaiian; these were sometimes used as business names.

XXVIII

Pai, Po, and Fong are family names with solid links to Daniel K. Pai. Pai is his Hawaiian family name [Paʻi] and his taken Chinese name [白]. Po [頗] is a Chinese surname. However, in this case, we believe it to be an abbreviated form of his mother's maiden name, Maʻinaʻaupo. Two influential people named Fong in Daniel K. Pai's life were Senator Hiram Fong, whom Daniel said was his uncle, and Henry Ah Fong, a foreman at the Parker Ranch; he was a mentor to Daniel Pai.

THE HISTORY OF PAI-LUM

Until the early seventies, the only thing anyone knew about Daniel K. Pai's background, aside from small bits and pieces about his training, was that he trained in Hawaiʻi. The only information anyone had came from stories told by Daniel K. Pai; there is no other first-hand information about his training. These stories often varied in detail depending on the audience or the specific point he was making while telling the story.

In 1980, when Daniel Pai was in Hawaiʻi to host the Third World Kuo-Shu Tournament, Patrick Hodges, a local martial arts teacher and historian, took him and Laura Austin (Ms. Austin was a Pai-Lum practitioner and Tao-Gar classmate of Mr. Hodges) out to dinner. In conversation, one of the many things Daniel Pai told Mr. Hodges was that he never told any of his students exactly where Pai-Lum came from and said that the foundation of his art was based on skills he learned from a Buddhist Nun. While there is no possible way to prove this is true, it is another data point.

It was not until around 1972 that any written history existed. A synopsis of the general history of Pai-Lum that most training halls had in the early part of the seventies is as follows:

> *"Legend has it that Daniel K. Pai began his martial arts training in Honolulu, Hawaiʻi, at age five. His grandfather taught him their family's martial arts system. At 12, he was sent to a White Lotus Temple on the northern coast of Okinawa where he trained in the art of Kempo. Upon returning to Hawaiʻi, he is said to have become a preeminent fighter in the islands."*

Most schools of Pai-Lum have a similar version of this history, along with varying details that are unique to each specific school; this means everyone has a slightly different version!

Daniel K. Pai's history, as taught at the White Lotus Kung-Fu Center in Albany, NY, was as follows:

> *"Daniel K. Pai was trained to fill the position of bill collector for his grandfather's import/export business (a position that necessitated martial expertise). He later served his country in both the Korean War and the Vietnam War in a very specialized capacity, which further tested and improved his fighting and survival abilities. Upon retirement from military service, he decided to put his capabilities to use for more peaceful purposes by teaching martial arts to the American public and emphasizing its use for survival in modern social conditions by developing physical, mental, and spiritual discipline."*

On the surface, this history would appear more plausible.

We consider these histories to be more Folklore than fact. Like many legends and myths, we believe them to be as correct in intent as they are wrong in detail. For example, while we believe Daniel Pai did some training in Okinawa when he was stationed in Japan, it is improbable that he was, at twelve years old, sent to Okinawa during wartime to train in the art of Kempo with his grandfather's friend! It is more plausible that he may have been sent to the Big Island at age sixteen because he was getting in trouble in Honolulu (getting in fights with US service members, for example). Even though he probably did not train in Okinawa as a teenager, he may have trained in Kempo (possibly Okinawan Kempo) while living on the Big Island.

These histories are very similar contextually to the Japanese concept of Tatemae. The Japanese concepts of Tatemae and Honne deal with the public and private truth: Tatemae, built in front of, or façade [建前], is the outward appearance based on position and what society expects; it is the publicly espoused, less than accurate story. Honne, true-sound [本音], is one's true inner feelings; it is the less glamorous, often hidden truth.

XXX

Pai-Lum Kung-Fu

An updated excerpt from

Dragon Tales

State University of New York at Albany, 1979

As it exists today, the Pai-Lum style of Kung-Fu is a unique cultural entity. It is a style of Kung-Fu whose practitioners are almost exclusively non-Chinese. Among the most highly trained practitioners of the style, only its late Grandmaster, Daniel K. Pai, is of Chinese descent.

The Pai-Lum style is a traditional Chinese-Hawaiian fabric cut and sewn to fit Westerners. Daniel K. Pai's ancestral trust was the preservation and continuation of his family style. Without a living biological heir to whom he could bequeath stewardship of this style, he had to adjust his teaching to the realization that he must ensure its adaptation to a culture vastly different from the one in which it originated.

Today, thirty-plus years after the passing of Grandmaster Daniel K. Pai, the Pai-Lum system is a body of American and International practitioners who share the methods and traditions of the style, despite locations ranging from North America, Hawai'i, Ireland, and Australia (just a few of the places where Pai-Lum practitioners congregate). There is enough interaction between the various Training Halls to ensure a sense of community and shared cultural uniqueness.

There is a consensus that practice of the art means that a person is different from others in a particular way. This sense of shared cultural "otherness" is called "being a Dragon" (Daniel K. Pai referred to his students as Dragons, a name most people in Pai-Lum have embraced). "Dragons" are proud of what makes them different and find that these qualities create a bond between them even when they have never met one another.

- Martin Pickands

XXXI

George Dillman, founder of U.S.A. Ryukyu Kempo, on what inspired him to seek out and train with Daniel K. Pai in the mid nineteen sixties. Mr. Dillman was the first person from the northeastern part of the US to train with Daniel K. Pai.

"Danny had been written up in the paper for putting a few guys in the hospital in the process of stopping a rape. He stepped in and "took them out"—put them in critical condition. When I heard about this I said, "Anybody who can do that, I want him to be my instructor."

- George Dillman

Prometheus: The George Dillman Story, 2014

"Four 100-pound blocks of ice are stacked on the canvas covered floor. A big, pudgy-looking man in black pajamas stands behind the ice. He rests the palm of his hand on the top block and goes through a kind of breathing exercise punctuated by gutteral growls. Suddenly, his whole body twitches and his hand raises a fraction of an inch, then strikes the ice. The ice shatters. . ."

- William Weir

Connecticut Magazine, September 1973

As the last demonstration at Aaron Banks' 1973 Oriental World of Self Defense, held at Madison Square Garden, this description was written by John T. McGee.

". . . Eat your heart out, said Danny Pai as he joked and clowned his way through his exhibition. He kept falling off a chair every time he reached up to break 1000 pounds of ice. Eventually, the Iron Arm descended. The ice was shattered, and the audience rose to their feet and cheered mightily, which was a fitting climax. . ."

- John T. McGee

Official Karate Magazine, October 1973

Patrick McCarthy, world-class author, researcher, teacher, and founder of the International Ryukyu Karate Research Society, had this to say when asked about Daniel K. Pai in an interview with Simon Keegan from Classical Karate & Jujutsu magazine in January 2016. Mr. McCarthy was a live-in student of Daniel K. Pai in the early seventies.

"Simon Keegan: Another of your early instructors, Daniel K. Pai, looks like an interesting character but is not so well known in the UK. What was he like?

Patrick McCarthy: Master Pai commanded a huge following during the 1970s as the founder of Pai Lum Kempo [a Hawaiian-Chinese based fighting art]. He was a charismatic instructor, a brutally powerful human being [understatement], a remarkably knowledgable and deeply spiritual person."

Classical Karate & Jujutsu magazine

Online magazine for the martial arts of

Japan, China & Okinawa, January 2016

- *Photo by Dave Everett*

*P*AI-*C*HIA *C*H'ÜAN

Chapter One

I GENERAL INFORMATION

WHAT IS PAI-CHIA CH'ÜAN AND PAI-LUM ?

Pai-Chia Ch'üan [白家拳] (pronounced bye-jya chywan) is a Mandarin dialect Chinese phrase that means Pai Family Fist, or boxing. It is a public name used to describe Pai-Lum Kung-Fu in general and our branch of the Pai Family Art in particular. This term is used primarily in the Pai Family training halls in southeastern Connecticut and upstate New York.

Pai-Lum is a modern style of Kung-Fu created by the late Daniel K. Pai, the founder and only recognized Grandmaster of that system. It is traditional martial arts adapted to today's needs, a fusion or amalgamation of Daniel K. Pai's martial knowledge, combining elements of Chinese, Okinawan, Hawaiian, and Japanese martial arts.

Pai-Lum is a principle-based martial art that integrates structural alignment and the dragon-style skills of coiling, compacting, and expanding. It is primarily a short-range or short-fist method. Constant forward motion, limb trapping, and sticking to an opponent are typical of the Pai method.

The root of Daniel K. Pai's system is said to have come from his grandfather. It is unknown what the system's original name was; it is believed to have been a method of dragon-style boxing. On many occasions, Daniel K. Pai stated that the

Daniel K. Pai teaching in Windgap, PA, 1985.

- Photo by Gary LaVallee

art he learned from his grandfather was called the White Dragon system. Daniel K. Pai is considered the orthodox founder of the Pai Family Art as we know it.

NAMES ASSOCIATED WITH DANIEL K. PAI'S TEACHINGS

Daniel K. Pai's teachings, which take place primarily over a thirty year span from 1963 to 1993, are known by various names, depending on the particular source and time. The most common of these names are Karate, Chinese Karate, Kempo, Pai-Lum Kung-Fu, Pai Family Kung-Fu, Pai-Chia Ch'üan [WG], White Dragon Fist Method, Pai-Lung Ch'üan-Fa [WG], White Lotus Style, or Bok-Leen Pai [CAN].

Pai-Lum was the first specific "System" name attached to Daniel K. Pai's teachings and the primary name he used when referring to his art. The official written name of Daniel K. Pai's art in the early nineteen seventies was Pai-Te Lung Ch'üan Shih-Yang [White Dragon Fist Style 白的龍拳式样]. It was also written as Pai-Lung Ch'üan-Fa [White Dragon Fist Method or Pai's Dragon Boxing 白龍拳法], usually shortened to Pai-Lung Ch'üan [White Dragon Fist 白龍拳]. The system name as written on some of the early certificates was Pai-Lung Kung-Fu K'ung-Shou Tao [White Dragon Skilled Empty Hand Way or White Dragon Kung-Fu Karate-Do 白龍功夫空手道].

WHAT DOES THE NAME PAI-LUM MEAN?

Pai-Lum is the name most often used when referring to the martial arts of Daniel K. Pai. There is, however, some controversy over the actual meaning of the name. Pai-Lum, often translated (incorrectly) as White Dragon, is, at first glance, made up of words from different dialects. It is an incorrect but common practice to mix dialects and spellings. There are many ways to romanize the

Pai-Lum Association patch from the early seventies.

various versions of the Chinese language. It would be best to have the Chinese characters and enough language understanding to translate them correctly.

It was common in Chinese and Hawaiian Pidgin English to combine phrases from different languages and dialects of the same language (early Hawaiian Pidgin combined Hawaiian, Cantonese, Portuguese, and American English), which may have also influenced the name. Some of the potential definitions are as follows:

White Dragon: Pai [WG] [Bok [CAN] or Pak [CAN] 白] means White; however, Lum [CAN] [Lin [WG] 林] means Forest, not Dragon [Lung [WG] 龍]. White Dragon [白龍] should be romanized as either Pai-Lung [WG] or Bok Loong [CAN]. While this translation does not appear to be accurate, there is a chance that Lum is simply an incorrect pronunciation of Lung or an incorrect romanization of the character 龍 [Lung]. Pai-Lung Ch'üan [WG] [White Dragon Boxing, Bailong Quan [PY]] is a commonly used name for Daniel Pai's system.

White Forest: Pai-Lum might be White Forest [白林]. Again, it may be a poor Romanization. Properly romanized, White Forest is Pai-Lin [WG] or Bok-Lum [CAN]. This translation could also be "Pai's Forest," meaning "Pai's martial artists" (In Chinese, the term Wu-Lin [WG] or Mo-Lum [CAN] means Martial Forest, a phrase used when referring to martial artists as a group).

Family Names: Pai and Lum are surnames (Pai being from the Mandarin dialect and Lum being from the Cantonese dialect). Pai-Lum may be a compound word combining two family names, "Pai" and "Lum." There are a large number of Chinese in Hawai'i with the surname Lum [Lim [CAN], Lin [WG]].

Pa'i-Lum: Another version of using family names combines the Hawaiian surname Pa'i and the Cantonese name Lum. Chinese and Hawaiian Pidgin English could have influenced this type of usage.

Pa'i Lima: The Hawaiian words Pa'i (to slap or crush with the palm) and Lima (hand or arm) may also have influenced the name Pai-Lum.

BOK LEEN PAI

Another term that became synonymous with Daniel K. Pai's teachings is Bok Leen Pai. Bok Leen Pai [CAN] [Pai Lien P'ai [WG] 白蓮派], which means White Lotus Sect/Style, began to be used in 1975 to represent all Pai Family Arts. It is part of Pai-Lum folklore that Daniel K. Pai's grandfather had sent him to a "White Lotus Monastery"[1]

Bok Leen Pai patch from the mid-seventies.

---

[1] While this is a widespread belief in many Pai-Lum schools, we could not verify that a White Lotus temple existed on the island of Okinawa.

[Bok Leen Ji CAN, Pai-Lien Ssu WG, Byaku Ren Ji JAP, 白蓮寺] on the north coast of Okinawa for approximately five years. He is said to have trained in a system of Kempo that some people in Pai-Lum refer to as White Lotus Kempo [Pai-Lien P'ai Ch'üan-Fa WG, 白蓮派拳法].

DANIEL K. PAI'S MARTIAL HISTORY 1965 - 1993

From the mid-nineteen sixties until his passing in nineteen ninety-three, Daniel K. Pai was a driving force in spreading Asian martial arts in North America. Initially teaching Karate and Kempo in the nineteen fifties and sixties, and his Kung-Fu method from the late sixties until his passing in nineteen ninety-three.

We do not know much about Daniel K. Pai's martial history before he became part of the North American martial arts scene in the mid-sixties. He quickly built a reputation as mean, rugged, knowledgable, and highly talented. There was a mystique about him; no one knew his background; he had a vast knowledge of the arts and taught things that no one else was teaching.

As a member of Robert Trias's United States Karate Association (USKA), Daniel K. Pai represented the Chinese arts as a regional chief instructor (Kempo) and a member of the "Technique, Style, and Research Board" representing the Shaolin arts; he was a highly respected competitor and referee at karate tournaments across the US.

Daniel K. Pai was among the first people in the continental US to publicly and openly teach Chinese-based martial arts to non-Chinese!

From 1965 to 1970, while living in Richmond, Virginia, he taught a combination of Okinawan Kempo (Goju-Ryu) and Chinese Kung-Fu, according to two students from that time,

Ed Parker, George Dillman, Jhoon Rhee and Daniel K. Pai, 1965.

- From the collection of George Dillman

Hampton Finney and Warren Cottrel.

People from other areas began to seek him out for martial training, with George Dillman (1965) and Thomas D. St. Charles (1967) among the first from the Northeast. This phenomenon of established martial artists seeking out Daniel Pai to train with him continued for his entire teaching career.

Publicly, his teachings were referred to as Karate, Chinese Karate, Kempo, and to a lesser degree, Kung-Fu; this term was just coming into wide spread use. The first public use of Daniel K. Pai's surname in a martial system or association was published in the Bridgeport Post newspaper on December 1, 1968. It states, *"Master Pai is a seventh degree black belt, master instructor for region 5 USKA, and president of the Pai Lim Chinese Karate Association."*

The nineteen seventies were very busy for Daniel K. Pai. When he wasn't teaching at his training hall, he conducted workshops, hosted or attended tournaments, and publicly demonstrated his art throughout the United States and Canada. These demonstrations were known as the *Masters' World of Kung-Fu and Karate*. They included many prominent martial artists demonstrating different aspects of their specific arts.

Business card for Daniel K. Pai's first school in Connecticut, 1970.
- From the collection of David L. Smith

In 1970, Daniel K. Pai moved to Bridgeport, Connecticut, and with the assistance of Thomas St. Charles, opened the "Pai Karate Institute." Around this time, due to the passing of one of his relatives (thought to be an uncle, a biological or martial relative), he inherited the rank and title of Grandmaster in his family's martial art method.

When Daniel K. Pai began teaching in New England, many people (students, instructors, and established teachers) sought to train with him. He also recruited some people he met at tournaments to train with him. The majority of people who became his students early on had previous training. Most had attained a brown belt or higher from various martial arts systems. Their "Pai-Lum" was built on top of the martial foundation they had at the time.

During these early days, when the "Pai-Lum Association" was formed, he concurrently served on the board of directors for the East Coast Karate Federation and as the chief instructor for the USKA (as was previously mentioned) and the Canadian Fire Dragon Association.

Fire Dragon Institute of Oriental Arts, 744 Park Street, Hartford, Connecticut.
- Photo by Ray Carpenter

Daniel K. Pai moved to Hartford, Connecticut in 1971, initially teaching at Farmington Ave. In the autumn of 1971, the training hall moved to 744 Park Street in Hartford. This location became the headquarters for the Pai-Lum Association and was officially named the "Fire Dragon Institute of Oriental Arts." At this point, the teachings began focusing primarily on Chinese-based skills. Techniques, drills, and form sequences were continually added to the quickly expanding curriculum of the Pai-Lum system. The teachings of Daniel K. Pai were becoming somewhat standardized and systematized, a necessary adjustment for teaching large groups of students with little or no previous experience. From then on, most warm-ups, fundamentals, form sequences, self-defense, and sparring were taught by a hierarchy of senior instructors, instructors, and student instructors. Daniel K. Pai oversaw and made adjustments and refinements as he saw fit.

These events were happening at the height of the Kung-Fu craze in America. The Kung-Fu television series, Hong Kong Kung-Fu movies, and Bruce Lee's popularity increased interest in Chinese Martial Arts. People with little or no martial background started training in the art of Pai-Lum Kung-Fu in large numbers. Fire Dragon and Pai-Lum training halls opened on the East Coast, Mid-West, and Eastern Canada.

This era peaked with over 2400 students in North America's fifty-plus Fire Dragon and Pai-Lum

Program cover for a "Masters World of Kung-Fu and Karate" demonstration in Kansas, 1973.

schools. Many of these schools were run by experienced instructors. Some, however, were operated by instructors with limited experience in the Pai-Lum System. Most of the instructors in these training halls taught the fundamentals they were familiar with within the framework of the growing Pai-Lum system. As a result of incredible growth, not having enough qualified instructors, and Daniel K. Pai teaching slightly different skills to his students, most schools of Pai-Lum today teach different interpretations of the Pai method.

With the closing of the Fire Dragon School on Park Street in 1975, the Pai-Lum Association moved to a new location on Prospect St. in Hartford. The name of the new training hall was the Bok Leen Pai Temple [White Lotus School Temple]; by late autumn, it had moved again to 12 Willard Street. Around this time, the Bok Leen Pai Temple began communicating and working earnestly with the Kuo-Shu Federation, ROC.

In 1976, Daniel Pai moved to Florida. He returned to the Northeast often, interacting with his students and teaching workshops at their schools. He lived in many places in Florida, opening schools where he resided and cultivating new students and instructors.

RECOGNITION BY THE REPUBLIC OF CHINA

It was very important to Daniel K. Pai that his Chinese family be recognized for their contribution to the martial arts. In 1974, he had his family's documents sent to the Republic of China to be verified. When this investigation was over, John Weninger held a banquet and martial arts demonstration in Allentown, PA. This banquet honored the Republic of China official, Consul General George Hsieh, who traveled from Washington, DC, to deliver documentation about and publicly announce that the Pai Family's martial heritage was officially recognized as a traditional Chinese martial art by the Republic of China. The demonstration culminated with Daniel K. Pai showcasing his, now-famous, ice break, which was well received by the Chinese official. After this event, George Younker remembers an elated Daniel K. Pai giving him a big hug and telling him it was one of the happiest days of his life.

Allenton, PA, 1974. Ice break demonstration.

Back row standing L to R - John Weninger, Republic of China Consul General George Hsieh, Phil Hunter, Seated - Janice Weninger, Vince Ward. Standing in front of the table on the right - Karen Tolczyk, Front - David Everett, Daniel K. Pai, unknown

- From the collection of John Weninger

In July 1976, Daniel K. Pai and a team of 13 people traveled to Taiwan, representing the White Dragon Martial Arts Society. They spent two grueling weeks demonstrating martial arts and training with members of the Kuo-Shu Association. The team was awarded a "Certificate of Merit" for superb achievement during the Kuo-Shu demonstrations in Taipei. Daniel K. Pai was named the North American representative for the Chinese Kuo-Shu Federation of the Republic of China.

Daniel K. Pai demonstrating an ice break at a Kuo-Shu event in Taiwan in the late nineteen seventies.

In 1978, the White Dragon Martial Arts Society's team participated in the 2nd World Kuo-Shu Tournament (Taipei, ROC). After this event, Daniel K. Pai was appointed delegate at large for the "Chinese Kuo-Shu Worldwide Promotion Association" (CKWPA).

The 3rd World Kuo-Shu Tournament was organized and hosted by Daniel K. Pai and his senior students in Honolulu, Hawai'i, in 1980.

In 1983, Daniel K. Pai's USA team participated in the 4th World Kuo-Shu Tournament (Taipei, ROC).

On November 10, 1983, Daniel K. Pai was elected Vice President of the 2nd executive board of the CKWPA.

In 1984, he organized and served as President of the CKWPA-USA Branch. The "Amateur Athletic Union" (AAU) appointed Daniel K. Pai as a delegate

*David L. Smith (International Kuo-Shu Referee), Maing Yul Jung
(USA Coach) and Daniel K. Pai (International Vice-President of
the Chinese Kuo-Shu Worldwide Promotion Association) at the 4th
World Kuo-Shu Championship in Taiwan, November, 1983.*

- Photo from the collection of David L. Smith

at large to the National AAU Kung Fu Committee and the "International Kung Fu Association" (IKFA), representing the Florida State Region in April 1984.

The Summer of 1989 saw Daniel K. Pai organizing and hosting the 6th World Kuo-Shu Tournament (Las Vegas, Nevada, USA), the last Major Kuo-Shu event personally overseen by Dr. Pai. His tenure as President of the "International Chinese Kuo-Shu Federation - USA" (formerly CKWPA-USA) ended in late 1990.

DANIEL K. PAI'S PASSING

Daniel K. Pai passed away on May 28, 1993, while traveling in the Dominican Republic. Since then, the arts of the Pai Family have been and continue to be taught, in many variations, by second, third, and fourth-generation Pai family instructors and teachers.

David L. Smith

David L. Smith began his martial training in 1966 in the Okinawan art of Isshin-Ryu Karate under Sensei Ralph Lindquist. Mr. Smith continued his training in college with various styles of Karate and began training in Judo under Sensei Kei Yoshida. Mr. Smith then began training under Sensei Louis S. Casamassa in Okinawan Karate, becoming Mr. Casamassa's first student to be promoted to Shodan.

David L. Smith
白靜林
Pai Ching-Lin
August 4, 1948 - May 20, 2023

April 11, 1970, Mr. Smith met Daniel K. Pai at a tournament sponsored by the Lafayette College martial arts club (Run by Mr. Smith and classmate Charles Powell). Later the same day, Daniel K. Pai invited Mr. Smith and Mr. Powell to train with him.

Lafayette karate tournament, April 11, 1970. L. to R. Louis Casamassa (kneeling), David L. Smith, George Dillman, and Daniel K. Pai.   - Photo by C. Powell

After graduating in 1970, Mr. Smith moved to Connecticut and began training with Grandmaster Pai. In the early seventies, Mr. Smith opened his first Pai-Lum training hall, Pai-Lung P'ai Wu-Shu Kuan [White Dragon Sect Martial Skills Hall 白龍派武術館], in Gales Ferry, CT.

Disciple/Adopted Grandson

In 1975, Mr. Smith became a disciple of Grandmaster Daniel K Pai. Around this time, he was also given the name Pai Tso-Ching [白坐靜]. In 1977, he was promoted to 4th Higher Level and accepted as an adopted Grandson[2] of Daniel K. Pai. In 1982, his name was changed to Pai Ching-Lin [白靜林].

---

2   Daniel K. Pai began giving some of his students Pai names in nineteen seventy two; some were even considered adopted Grandchildren. However, it was not until the later part of the seventies that a handful of people were made adopted Grandchildren of Daniel K. Pai with the sole purpose of perpetuating the Pai martial tradition. A grandchild council was formed. The initial four Grandsons on this council were David Everett - Vice President; John Weninger - Executive Vice President; David L. Smith - Secretary; and Ron Lydestad - Sergeant at arms.

Lafayette karate tournament, April 11, 1970. David L. Smith and Daniel K. Pai.

During the 1980 Third World Kuo-Shu Tournament in Hawai'i, Mr. Smith was responsible for organizing and running the competition part of the event.

In June 1982, Mr. Smith was named chief instructor for the Pai-Lum system in the northeastern part of the US and was one of three people authorized to issue rank and teaching certification in the Pai-Lum system.

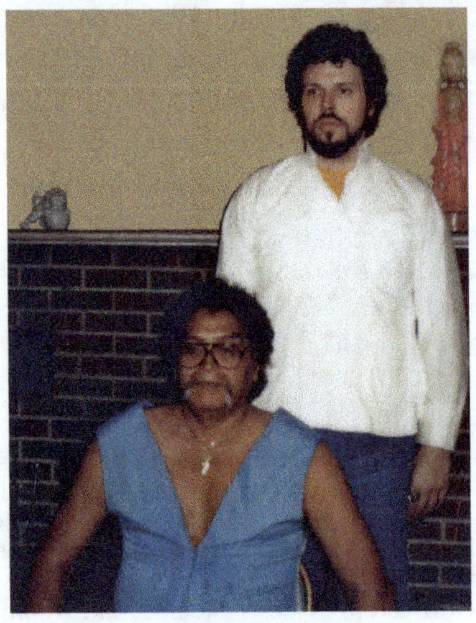

Daniel K. Pai and David L. Smith
1983, Windgap, PA

Group photo for the International Referee training for the 4th World Kuo-Shu tournament. Kaohsiung, Taiwan, ROC on October 28 1983.

- From the collection of David L. Smith

TEACHERS IN TAIWAN

In November 1983, Mr. Smith attended referee training in Taiwan, ROC, and was certified as an International Kuo-Shu referee. He participated in the 4th World Kuo-Shu Tournament as a referee and alternate member/representative of Daniel K. Pai. While attending referee training, Mr. Smith was introduced to many famous masters and was fortunate to train with a handful of these men:

Ch'en Chin-Yuan 陳金源 (South Shaolin Eighteen Bronze-Man System)

Hsieh Hsin-Keng 謝辛庚 (T'ung-I T'ang Wu-Yi)

Wang Tsao-Yang 王朝陽 (Southern Lohan)

Ma Tsao-Jih 馬朝日 (Feeding Crane, Golden Eagle Boxing)

Lin I-Sheng 林益生 (Fukien Yung Ch'un Boxing)

Chou Keng-Hsin 周庚辛 (Shaolin Ch'in-Na)

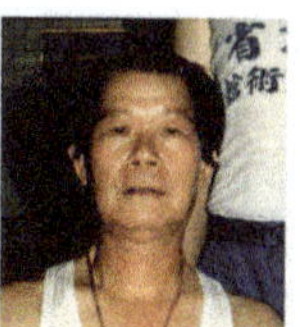

Ch'en Chin-Yuan
陳金源

Hsieh Hsin-Keng
謝辛庚

Wang Tsao-Yang
王昭陽

Ma Tsao-Jih
馬朝日

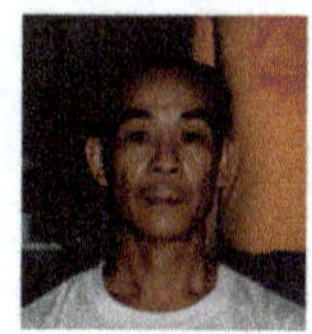

Lin I-Sheng
林益生

Chou Keng-Hsin
周庚辛

General Information

Mr. Smith became a disciple of Ch'en Chin-Yuan, Grandmaster of the South Shaolin Eighteen Bronze-Man System. Mr. Smith is responsible for introducing this art in the United States. In addition to the original method of Ch'en Lao-Shih, Mr. Smith adapted Pai-Lum techniques to the Eighteen Bronze-Man training dummy (AKA the iron dummy). He developed new drills and training routines, essentially creating a Pai method of iron dummy training.

While in Taiwan, Mr. Smith lived and spent much of his time with Hsieh Hsin-Keng. Mr. Hsieh was a famous martial artist that trained primarily under Han Ch'ing-T'an [韓慶堂] (Northern Shaolin, Ch'in-Na), Wang Chueh-Jen [王珏鑫] (T'ien-Shan P'ai), and Lo Tzu-Lung [羅子龍] (T'ung-I T'ang Wu-Yi, T'ien-Shan P'ai).

Under Hsieh Lao-Shih, Mr. Smith trained in all aspects of the martial arts and learned about Chinese and Taiwanese culture. He is listed in Master Hsieh's T'ung-I T'ang lineage as his number 9 student.

These were enlightening events in Mr. Smith's martial career.

Ch'en Chin-Yuan
and
David L. Smith

Hsieh Hsin-Keng
and
David L. Smith

MARCIA L. PICKANDS

Marcia Pickands (maiden name Kellsey) began her martial arts training in 1972. Her introduction to Pai-Lum was attending a demonstration by Daniel K. Pai and his students at the University of Connecticut and subsequently joining the UConn Kung-Fu Club. The initial classes were taught by Daniel Pai, with the remainder of the semester being taught by instructors and student instructors in Daniel Pai's school. She liked the people and the workout and stayed in the club. The next time she met Daniel Pai was early in 1973; he invited her to train at the Park Street School in Hartford.

MARCIA PICKANDS
白白鶴
Pai Pai-He
March 3, 1954 - January 4, 2016

Within six months, she led classes and eventually became a live-in student of Daniel K. Pai. Ms. Pickands initiated a program called "Recognizing Violence in its Perspective," an ongoing program promoting the values of martial arts training. She was instrumental in developing and getting this program into the Hartford school system.

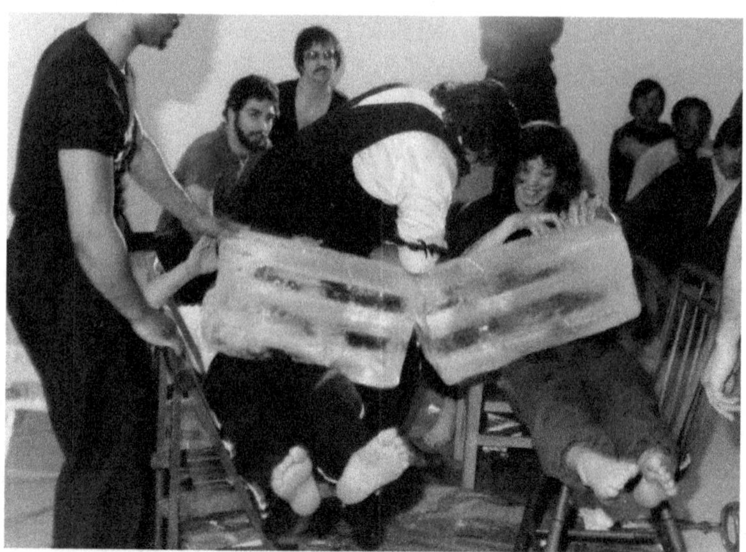

Daniel K. Pai breaking a 200 pound slab of ice laid across two students, at the school opening demonstration for the White Lotus Kung-Fu Center in Albany, NY in 1979.

- Photo by Martin Pickands

With Daniel Pai moving to Florida in 1976, Ms. Pickands continued her training with David Everett at his school in West Hartford, in addition to her training with Grandmaster Pai.

In 1978, she moved to Delmar, NY with her husband Martin. Every week she commuted back and forth between Albany and Hartford (to teach sparring class) until she opened the White Lotus Kung-Fu Center in 1979.

On 4/23/79 Ms. Pickands was accepted as a disciple, and in 1980, she became the second adopted Grandaughter of Daniel K. Pai, and was given the name Pai Pai-He [Bok-Hok White Crane 白鶴].

She was one of the first people in the Pai-Lum system to attain senior instructor status who had no previous martial arts experience before training in Pai-Lum.

ESTABLISHMENT OF A BRANCH SYSTEM AND FORMAL NAMING

With the passing of Daniel K. Pai, David L. Smith, in agreement with and authorized by Grandmaster Pai, became the head of a branch system of the Pai family arts. This branch of the Pai-Lum system was initially referred to as Pai-Chia Ch'üan [Pai Family Fist 白家拳] and is currently known as Pai-Lin Ch'üan [White Forest Fist 白林拳].

PAI-LIN CH'ÜAN

Pai-Lin Ch'üan was formally established by David L. Smith upon the passing of Daniel K. Pai in 1993, though not officially named until 2000. In a formal ceremony on May 30, 2000, at the end of a seven-year mourning period for the passing of his teacher, David L. Smith announced the name of his branch system. The formal, trademarked name is Pai-Lin. That name may stand alone or be expressed as Pai-Lin followed by Ch'üan, Kung-Fu, Wu-Kung, Wu-Te, Wu-Tao, or other generic terms meaning "martial art" system. Pai-Lin Ch'üan is considered to be born of the early (1970-1973) martial teachings of Grandmaster Daniel K. Pai; it is Mr. Smith's interpretation and expression of Pai-Lum. In addition, there are influences from several 2nd generation Pai family teachers and elements of other martial arts systems. Pai-Lin Ch'üan is a principle-based art that is continually growing and evolving.

Pai-Chia Wu-Kung Hui

The Pai Family Martial Training Association [Pai-Chia Wu-Kung Hui 白家武功會] is an organization devoted to the perpetuation of traditional martial arts.

The primary arts taught at this association are Pai Family Boxing [Pai-Chia Ch'üan 白家拳] (Pai-Lum), White Forest Boxing [Pai-Lin Ch'üan 白林拳], and the South Shaolin Eighteen Bronze-Man Method [Nan Shao-Lin Shih-Pa T'eng-Jen Fa 南少林十八銅人法]. The Eighteen Bronze-Man Method comprises the traditional method of Ch'en Chin-Yuan and the Pai method developed by Mr. Smith in 1984. In addition, elements from many other teachers are practiced, perpetuated, and represented by this association.

Pai-Shou Athletic Association letterhead 1980 - 1987

This association grew out of the Pai-Shou Athletic Association [Pai-Shou T'i-Yu Hui 白手體育會], a group of North Eastern Pai-Lum schools that worked closely together from 1980 to 1987; it comprised the Pai-Shou Athletic Association (headquarters), New London CT (head instructor David L. Smith), and two independent schools; the White Lotus Kung-Fu Center, Albany NY (head instructor Marcia Pickands), and Hsin Lung Kwan, Worcester MA (head instructor Phil Hunter).

David L. Smith with Disciples
Pai-Shou Athletic Association, New London, CT 2002

- Photo by Pete Stoddard

 General Information

Since the early nineteen nineties, the Pai Family Martial Training Association comprised two active training halls: Pai-Shou Athletic Association (Ching-Lin Kuan) in New London, CT, and Ying-Hao Kuan in Hoosick Falls, NY. In addition to these active training halls, Daniel Anhalt and William Luciano taught martial arts clubs and classes.

The Next Generation

On September 13, 2014, at Ying-Hao Wu-Kung Kuan in Hoosick Falls, New York. Mr. David L. Smith and Ms. Marcia L. Pickands accepted both Daniel Anhalt and William Luciano as third generation, "inside the room" disciples in the lineage of Daniel K. Pai and co-inheritors of Mr. Smith's branch of the Pai family art, formally passing on the responsibility for perpetuating the Pai Family Martial Training Association's understanding of Pai-Lum, Pai-Chia Ch'üan and Pai-Lin Ch'üan to both of them equally and independently.

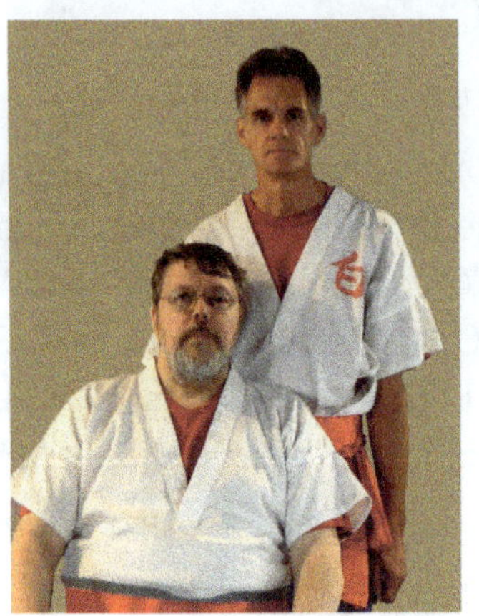

David L. Smith
with
Daniel Anhalt

David L. Smith
with
William Luciano

At the same ceremony, William Luciano and Michael Rothermel were named co-inheritors to Mr. Smith's South Shaolin Eighteen Bronze-Man System branch. Both are equally and independently responsible for perpetuating the traditional Ch'en Family method and Mr. Smith's Pai Family adaptations.

In October 2018, Andrew St. John began teaching elements of Pai-Chia Ch'üan and Pai-Lin Ch'üan at his private training hall in Schenectady, NY.

Daniel K. Pai demonstrating his famous ice break.

- Photo from the collection of John Weninger

Chapter Two

II MARTIAL ART DEFINITIONS

WU-SHU, KUO-SHU, WU-KUNG, KUNG-FU, AND KEMPO

This chapter will discuss some basic information about Chinese-based martial arts. Wu-Shu 武術, Kuo-Shu 國術, Wu-Kung 武功, Kung-Fu 功夫, and Kempo 拳法 are popular terms used to describe Chinese martial arts.

Wu-Shu means martial art, craft, or skill. Traditional Wu-Shu describes all martial arts from China. Contemporary Wu-Shu is China's modern, performance-based art; it combines gymnastics and generic, martial art-like skills. While contemporary Wu-Shu has outstanding physical training, it has little or no martial use.

Kuo-Shu means national art, craft, or skill. Its use became popular in the nineteen twenties during the early days of the Republic of China. Today, it is the prominent term for Chinese martial arts in Taiwan and is used by martial artists worldwide affiliated with teachers and methods from Taiwan or pre-communist China.

Wu-Kung means martial training. A term used to describe martial arts generally, it is also more indicative of the actual practice of martial skills.

Kung-Fu means a skill accomplished through time and effort. A generic term for Chinese martial arts used since the early 1960s. Kung-Fu is also a generic term for exercise.

Kempo, or Kenpo, is a Japanese pronunciation of the Chinese term Ch'üan-Fa [Fist Method 拳法]. It is used throughout Japan and most of the Western world to describe arts heavily influenced by Chinese martial methods.

WHAT DOES KUNG-FU MEAN?

Technically, Kung-Fu does not mean martial art. Kung-Fu [功夫] (pronounced Gung-Fu) means a skill acquired through time and effort. It also describes someone adept at a particular skill. In martial arts, it defines a higher level of proficiency associated with martial training.

The first use of Kung-Fu by a Westerner was by Jean Joseph Marie Amiot, a French Jesuit missionary stationed in Beijing during the late 1700s. He used the term to describe the martial arts of China. The first use of Kung-Fu in English literature was John Dudgeon's 1895 essay "Kung Fu, or Tauist Medical Gymnastics." This use of the term Kung-Fu described Taoist exercises and breathing skills. Today, this would be referred to as Ch'i-Kung [氣功].

Later in the 1950s, Kung-Fu became associated with Chinese martial arts in San Francisco, California. An art called "Sil-Lum Gung-Fu CAN [Shaolin Kung-Fu 少林功夫]" was taught by recent Hong Kong immigrants. Up until this point in the United States, the martial arts of China were referred to as Chinese Boxing, Chinese Karate, or Chinese Kempo, depending on the source.

By the late 1960s, Kung-Fu had become the primary name used in the United States when describing Chinese martial arts. Bruce Lee's impact on American television, the "Kung-Fu" television series, and the Hong Kong "Kung-Fu" movies, which were very popular in the early nineteen seventies, solidified the term Kung-Fu.

The Merriam-Webster dictionary defines Kung-Fu as a form of fighting without weapons developed in China: a Chinese martial art. In this context, the term "Kung-Fu" will be used in this publication.

WHAT IS KUNG-FU?

Kung-Fu is a refined method of self-defense that is Chinese in origin. Every system of Kung-Fu has certain areas in which it excels or has different ways of doing techniques that are particular to its system. All systems of Kung-Fu have certain things in common. For instance, in its most basic form, each system will contain at least four areas of martial development: kicking, striking, felling, and controlling. Hence, the saying that describes the elements of Kung-Fu:

"T'i, Ta, Shuai, Na"

Kicking, Striking, Felling, Controlling

[踢 打 摔 拿]

1. Kicking [T'i 踢] - Any method of hitting using the lower part of the body as a weapon (from the waist down).

2. Striking [Ta 打] - Any method of hitting using the upper part of the body as a weapon (from the waist up).

3. Felling [Shuai 摔] - Any method of putting an opponent on the ground (throwing, sweeping, pushing, tackling, etc.).

4. Controlling [Na 拿] - Any method of catching, holding, and restraining an opponent (a significant part of controlling is joint locking).

Other specialized skills that most systems contain but which are generally considered higher level are weaponry [wu-ch'i 武器], breath/energy training [ch'i-kung 氣功], and vital point attacking [tien-hsueh [WG], dim yut [CAN] 點穴 or tien-mai [WG], dim mak [CAN] 點脈].

Traditionally, martial arts were used for combat and personal defense. It was not until the 20th century that martial arts practice for health or sport became popular. In the nineteen twenties, the Republic of China promoted martial arts training to help strengthen the Chinese people. They began referring to their traditional martial arts as Kuo-Shu [National Art 國術], a tradition still followed in Taiwan, ROC.

Throughout history, Kung-Fu developed from many sources. It would take multiple volumes to document this correctly. In modern times (for convenience), it is generally taught that Kung-Fu was developed by two primary sources: Warriors and Scholars.

Warriors: These people relied on their martial ability for survival and developed sound, effective fighting techniques and theories. Military men, bodyguards, police, and mercenaries are among those who fit into this category.

Scholars: While these people used martial arts to defend themselves when needed, they did not rely on these skills for survival. A preference of these people was to combine fighting skills, internal strength development, and health-giving exercises. Monks and people from wealthy families fit in this category. Both had an essential role in developing the many qualities we train for today: self-defense, health, discipline, and mind/body coordination.

NAMES FOR CHINESE MARTIAL ARTS

Some of the proper names for Chinese martial arts and martial arts categories are as follows:

Wu-Shu	Martial Craft/Art	武術
Kuo-Shu	National Craft/Art	國術
Wu-Kung	Martial Skill/Training	武功
Chung-Kuo Ch'üan	Chinese Fist/Boxing	中國拳
Ch'üan-Shu	Fist Craft/Art	拳術
Ch'üan-Fa	Fist Method	拳法
Wu-I	Martial Art	武藝
Shuai-Chiao	Wrestling	摔角
Ch'in-Na	Seize & Control	擒拿
Wai-Chia Ch'üan	External Family Fist	外家拳
Nei-Chia Ch'üan	Internal Family Fist	内家拳
Pei-Ch'üan	Northern Fist	北拳
Nan-Ch'üan	Southern Fist	南拳
Kempo [JAP] (Japanese)	Fist Method	拳法
Tu-di [OK] (Okinawan)	T'ang (China) Hand	唐手
Kun Tao [HOK] (Indonesian)	Fist Way	拳道

CATEGORIZING KUNG-FU [功夫]

The curriculum of Pai-Chia Ch'üan contains techniques and training methods from many martial arts systems. These systems originated in different parts of China, Taiwan, Hawai'i, Okinawa, and Japan. Systems from China and Taiwan are traditionally associated with one or more of the following categories: northern, southern, soft, hard, internal, or external. Systems with a Chinese/Okinawan, Chinese/Hawaiian, or Chinese/Japanese heritage are considered Kempo.

These categories are somewhat general and do not accurately describe many Chinese-based martial systems as taught today (most of today's methods are combinations of many arts). However, these categories parallel traditionally accepted beliefs and are orthodox teachings. In some cases, they may give a little insight into where a particular system might have originated.

GEOGRAPHIC CATEGORIES OF CHINESE MARTIAL ARTS

Geographically, there are many ways to categorize martial arts in China. The most popular is the separating of arts into northern or southern systems. Martial arts may also be grouped by province or village. Another popular way is to associate systems with culturally significant mountains. Such as Sung Shan [嵩山], where the Shaolin Temple [少林寺] is located, and Wu-Tang Shan [武当山], purported by some to be where Nei-Chia Ch'üan (internal martial arts) was developed.

NORTHERN - SOUTHERN [北 - 南 PEI - NAN]

The Yang-Tzu River is the primary reference when dividing Chinese martial arts into northern and southern methods. Northern styles differ from Southern styles in several fundamental ways, primarily for geographic and cultural reasons. A popular but inaccurate definition of the differences between northern and southern martial arts states that Northern styles are more adept with leg techniques and Southern styles are more proficient with hand techniques. From this comes the saying:

"Pei-T'ui ... Nan-Ch'üan"

Northern Legs ... Southern Fists

[北腿...南拳]

These generalizations come from many of the Shaolin arts which have northern and southern branches. Many texts from the late nineteenth and early twentieth century promoted these ideas. Two prominent organizations that promoted the martial skills of the north in the early twentieth century are the "Ching-Wu Athletic Association"[精武體育會] of Shanghai [上海] and the "Central Kuo-Shu Institute" [中央國術館] of Nanking [南京]. Today, the most popular information about northern-style martial arts comes from these two sources.

                    Martial Art Definitions

The Ching-Wu Association, well known for the many northern systems taught there, was the first Chinese martial arts organization to teach publicly, wear specific training uniforms, and issue certificates for martial arts courses completed. Arts taught there included the Lost Track system of Huo Yuan-Chia [Mi-Tsung Ch'üan 迷蹤拳]; the Eagle Claw system of Ch'en Tzu-Cheng [Ying Chiao P'ai 鷹爪派]; the Seven Star Praying Mantis system of Luo Kuang-Yu [Ch'i-Hsing T'ang-Lang Ch'üan 七星螳螂拳]; and the Wu Style T'ai-Chi Ch'üan of Wu Chien-Ch'üan [Wu-Shi T'ai-Chi Ch'üan 吳氏太極拳].

The Nanking Central Kuo-Shu Institute was a government-run entity explicitly created for the research and advancement of martial arts. At this institute, a Northern Long fist [Pei Ch'ang-Ch'üan,北長拳] curriculum was created by combining elements and training routines from many different northern methods.

NORTHERN SYSTEMS [PEI-CH'ÜAN 北拳]

Northern China is where Chinese martial arts began. One of the oldest recorded northern systems (aside from wrestling) was developed by the first emperor of the Sung Dynasty (A.D. 960 - 1127). This art became known as T'ai-Tzu Ch'ang-Ch'üan [Great Ancestor's Long Boxing 太祖長拳]. This system may have influenced many later methods, such as T'ai-Chi Ch'üan [Grand Ultimate Fist 太極拳].

In modern times the name Ch'ang-Ch'üan [long fist/boxing 長拳] is a generic term used to describe most Northern methods and any long-range technique or system that specializes in them.

A core training method for northern long-fist is to execute techniques using a full range of motion coordinating the simultaneous extension of both the driving leg and striking arm as the stance is completed. This practice trains the ability to create and issue energy, at any range, during the execution of a technique.

Northern style training routines are generally considered long-range and include many techniques. Three significant characteristics attributed to northern training forms are:

1. Highly refined leg maneuvers/kicking skills.

2. Physically demanding training sequences with complex, almost acrobatic techniques.

3. Primarily middle to long-range techniques.

While Northern styles appear to prefer long-range techniques, one should keep in mind that many of these methods are medium to long-range in training and short to medium-range when applied. Two such arts are Eight-Trigram Palm [Pa-Kua Chang 八卦掌] and Eight-Extremities Fist [Pa-Chi Ch'üan 八極拳]. Interestingly, one of the most comprehensive Ch'in-Na systems is found within the Eagle Claw System [Ying-Chiao P'ai 鷹爪派].

Three northern style training routines that have been adapted for use in Pai-Chia Ch'üan are Lien-Pu Ch'üan [training footwork set 練步拳, sometimes referred to as continuous steps set 連步拳], Tuan-Ta Ch'üan [short strike set 短打拳] and Pa-Pu Ch'üan [jumping steps set 拔步拳]. In the Pai based arts, they are called Flowing Form Two, Flowing Form Three, and Flowing Water, respectively.

SOUTHERN SYSTEMS [NAN-CH'ÜAN 南拳]

Southern systems are generally no-nonsense martial arts designed strictly for fighting. Many of today's popular southern systems were developed during the later part of the Ch'ing dynasty (AD 1644-1911) and the Republic's early years. These methods trace their origins to a southern Shaolin temple in Fukien province. Some of these systems were developed and used by revolutionaries and secret societies for the primary purpose of overthrowing the Ch'ing dynasty's Manchu [Man-chou tsu 滿洲族] rulers and returning power to the Han [Han tsu 漢族] Chinese, rulers of the Ming Dynasty [A.D. 1368-1644].

Southern systems can be divided into two major groups, those preferring a low, wide horse stance and those preferring a higher, narrower, toe-in horse stance (popular in Fukien province). Generally, systems that prefer a wide horse stance specialize in middle-range techniques and powerful thrusting strikes. Many of these systems were northern methods adapted by the southern Chinese. An excellent example of this type of system is Hung Family Boxing [Hung-Chia Ch'üan 洪家拳]. Systems preferring a narrow horse stance generally specialized in short-range techniques. Sometimes called "Short Fist,"

          Martial Art Definitions

these systems prefer quick, accurate strikes usually aimed at nerve centers. A good example of this type of system is Fukien White Crane Boxing [Fukien Pai-He Ch'üan 福建白鶴拳], one of the older, more refined southern methods.

Southern training routines are characterized by solid, rooted stance-work and quick, powerful strikes and are usually preceded by a salutation. Some southern training sets and most salutations were full of hidden meanings that relayed secret messages or identified the martial artist's group. Three significant characteristics of southern training forms are:

1. Heavy emphasis on hand techniques.

2. Solid, rooted stance-work.

3. Short to middle range techniques.

Two of the southern style sets style training sets that have been adapted for use in Pai-Chia Ch'üan are Liu-Chia Ch'üan [Liu family fist 劉家拳] and Kung-Tzu Fu-Hu Ch'üan [I pattern taming tiger fist 工字伏虎拳]. In the Pai family arts, these sets are called Flowing Form One and Taming Tiger.

THE QUALITIES OF CHINESE MARTIAL ARTS

It is also popular to classify Chinese Martial Arts by their martial qualities. The four most discussed qualities are hard, soft, internal, and external.

SOFT STYLE VS. HARD STYLE

Within most systems, there is both hard and soft style training. Defensive preferences differentiate soft styles and hard styles. Soft styles prefer passive defensive methods such as yielding, redirecting, and parrying. These methods usually "draw" an opponent in and counter-attack them when they are over-extended and off-balance. Hard styles use aggressive blocking methods to destroy an opponent's weapon(s) and collapse their defense.

EXTERNAL VS. INTERNAL STRENGTH

In Wu-Kung (martial training), there are two types of energy or strength used: Li [力] and Chin [勁]. Li is raw muscular strength built up by rigorous physical exercise. It is considered an external strength. Chin is a more refined and relaxed energy or strength that is produced by combining Li, Ch'i [breath/internal energy 氣], and I [intent 雷]. It is considered internal energy or strength. There are many types of Chin, the most common being Fa-Chin [issuing energy 發勁], T'ing Chin [listening energy 聽勁], T'an-Chin [elastic or spring energy 彈勁], and Nien Chin [adhering energy 粘勁].

EXTERNAL

External systems [Wai-Chia Ch'üan 棍家拳] generally work from hard to soft. Initial training is devoted to developing Li in the limbs and martial techniques. As one becomes more skillful and competent in the fundamental techniques and theories, there is a gradual shift of importance to the development of Ch'i and Chin. Shaolin systems and their offshoots are often purported to be external systems.

INTERNAL

Internal systems [Nei-Chia Ch'üan 內家拳] generally work from soft to hard. Initial training is devoted to the development of the torso (opening and closing the hips and shoulders), and both Ch'i and Chin. As time progresses, martial techniques and how to apply Chin to them become an increasingly important part of training for these systems. Internal systems are often thought to be associated with Wu-Tang Mountain.

INTERNAL/EXTERNAL

Internal/External systems place equal emphasis on the development of both Li and Chin right from the start. Most of today's martial methods train in this fashion.

In summing up the differences between external and internal systems, it is safe to say that the only real differences are the methods for developing and issuing force during the initial training years.

INTERNAL - EXTERNAL IN PAI-CHIA CH'ÜAN

We prefer to use the terms internal and external to describe different levels of martial arts as well as different methods; external represents the lower or more elementary level of Wu-Kung, and internal represents the higher or more refined. Therefore, in Wu-Kung, regardless of the system or style, one must begin from the external and patiently and systematically progress inwards to the internal.

     Martial Art Definitions

Incorrect Definitions of Internal and External

In many Chinese martial arts systems, it is commonly taught that Shaolin arts are external and Wu-Tang arts are internal. This concept was used for the first time at the Nanking Central Kuo-Shu Institute in 1928. The accuracy of this information was debunked by martial historian Táng Háo [唐豪] in the nineteen-thirties, but it is still taught today.

Other incorrect teachings are:

1. The terms refer to the origins of these systems: Shaolin is external (wai) because it is Buddhist, and Buddhism came from outside (external) into China. Wu-Tang is internal (nei) because it is Taoist, and Taoism came from inside (internal) China.

2. Any hard or fast movements are external; softer and slower movements are internal.

3. Overpowering and destroying the enemy is external; neutralizing and using the opponent's energy against them is internal.

Chinese Arts in Neighboring Countries

Kempo and Kuntao are examples of arts that combine Chinese methods with martial arts from different cultures. We consider these arts to be branches of traditional Wu-Shu.

Kempo [拳法 Ch'üan-Fa]

Kempo [JAP], also spelled Kenpo, is a Japanese term for Chinese martial arts, which, in Mandarin Chinese, is pronounced Ch'üan-Fa. Kempo means "fist method," though it is sometimes interpreted as "fist law." It is a term that has been used by the United States Karate Association (USKA) since its inception (1948) to describe all Chinese martial arts and arts with a heavy Chinese influence.

As an art, Kempo can be most accurately described as a fundamental Chinese martial art that has been transplanted to another culture and has grown and developed on its own, despite being separated from its source. Basic Kempo is generally an external martial art that relies on physical strength, speed, and body conditioning. Kempo can be either northern, southern, external, or Internal, depending on the Chinese system or systems on which it is based.

There are many different styles of Kempo; they can be divided into four major groups: Chinese, Okinawan, Japanese, and Hawaiian.

CHINESE KEMPO: This is essentially Chinese martial arts described from a Japanese perspective. In the United States, this has come to mean any Chinese or Chinese-based martial art.

OKINAWAN KEMPO: To-de [JAP], China hand [Tuudi [OK], Tang-shou [WG], 唐手] is a martial art that combines Chinese martial arts with Okinawa's indigenous percussive striking art, [Ti'gwa [OK] 手小]. To-de is known in the West as Okinawa-te [Uchinaa-di [OK] 沖縄手] and Okinawan Kempo (te or de is Japanese for hand, ti or di is Okinawan for hand). To-de, alternately pronounced Kara-te, eventually became known as To-de Jutsu, or Karate Jutsu [JAP] [唐手術] and varied from one teacher to another. These arts are the predecessors of modern Okinawan Karate and Japanese Karate-Do [JAP] [空手道].

JAPANESE KEMPO: Shorin-Ji Kempo [JAP] means Shaolin Temple Fist Method [Shao-Lin Ssu Ch'üan-Fa [WG] 少林寺拳法]. Founded by Doshin So (1911-1980) in 1947, Shorin-Ji Kempo is a Japanese-based martial art that claims to descend from the Shao-Lin Temple.

HAWAIIAN KEMPO: The broad definition of Hawaiian Kempo is any Chinese or Chinese-based martial art (including Okinawan Kempo) practiced or developed outside of Chinese culture in Hawai'i. As a particular method or system, Hawaiian Kempo usually implies any martial art that traces its lineage to James Mitose (Kosho Shorei-Ryu Kenpo) or William K.S. Chow (Kara-Ho Kenpo). Two additional branches influenced primarily by the teachings of William K.S. Chow are Kajukenbo, as created and taught by Adriano Emperado, Joe Holck, Peter Choo, Frank Ordonez, and Clarence Chang, and American Kenpo-Karate, as taught by Edmund K. Parker. These arts have branched off into several individual schools. Because of the martial diversity in Hawai'i, it is not uncommon to find elements of other martial arts such as Kung-Fu, Eskrima, Jujitsu, Western Boxing, and Lua in the various Kempo methods. It would not be out of line to consider the modern Kung-Fu systems of Daniel K. Pai (Pai-Lum Kung-Fu) and Al Dacascos (Wun Hop Kuen Do [CAN]) as independent branches of Hawaiian Kempo.

Martial Art Definitions

KEMPO IN PAI-CHIA CH'ÜAN

We believe that Daniel K. Pai had training in Chinese, Okinawan, Japanese, and Hawaiian Kempo methods; this is evident in the core fundamentals of the Pai-based arts.

In Pai-Chia Ch'üan, the term Kempo is used to describe basic, fundamental martial techniques (such as closed fist basics) that are used as a foundation for higher-level skills and training forms of Chinese/Okinawan heritage.

Two Kempo (Okinawan) training forms practiced in our branch of Pai-Chia Ch'üan are Tensho [JAP,] [rotating palms, Chuan Chang [WG] 轉掌] and Seisan [JAP,] [thirteen hands, Shih San Shou [WG] 十三手]. Tensho is sometimes referred to as Yun-Ch'i [WG,] [Vital Breath 蘊氣] by Pai family practitioners.

KUNTAO [拳道 CH'ÜAN-TAO]

Kuntao [HOK] is a Hokkien dialect term for Chinese martial arts. In Mandarin, it is pronounced Ch'üan-Tao [WG] [fist way, 拳道]. Kuntao is essentially Chinese martial arts as practiced by the Chinese communities of Southeast Asia (Indonesia, Malaysia, Singapore, and the Philippines). Many styles of Kuntao contain elements of the Southeast Asian Silat methods.

Grandmaster Daniel K. Pai demonstrating a classical Pao-Ch'üan Salute
- Photo by Christopher Lee Helton

Chapter Three

III MARTIAL ETIQUETTE

ETIQUETTE WHAT DOES IT MEAN?

Etiquette, by definition, means "Any code of behavior and courtesy." In martial arts, proper etiquette requires that much respect is paid to the teachers (past and present), the training hall, visitors, and classmates (senior and junior). This is an essential vehicle for learning!

THE MARTIAL TRAINING HALL [WU-KUNG KUAN 武功馆]

Kuan [WG] [or Kwoon [CAN]] means hall. In the context that martial artists use this phrase, it means "Martial (training) Hall" or "Wu-Kuan." Examples of how this is used are Pai-Chia Wu-Kung Kuan (Pai Family Martial Training Hall) or Pai-Chia Kuan (Pai Family Hall).

The Kuan is the physical center of a martial arts school. It is a place where hard work, respect, and tradition are as important as, or more important than, the martial technique.

The Kuan is not just a gymnasium used to work out. There are no set dimensions, floor types, or training equipment that are inherent in every Kuan. What defines a Kuan is the lineage, traditions, teacher, students, and training methods. Every one of the over 300 styles of kung-fu is different and unique in all of these categories.

Figure 1

Ancestral Shrine at the Ying-Hao Martial Training Hall (Ying-Hao Wu-Kung Kuan)

In most traditional Wu-Kuan, there is an ancestral shrine (Figure 1). Often called a Kung-Fu shrine, the actual term for this shrine is Shen T'ai [WG] [Sun Toi [CAN] 神檯], or Spirit table. The Shen T'ai is the spiritual center of a Kuan. Typically, an ancestral shrine will have an incense burner, candles, cups filled with various things (such as water, grain, and salt), statues, flowers, fruits, and pictures of significant figures in the lineages of the systems taught in the Kuan.

When you are in the Kuan, you should devote your entire time to training. The main area of a Kuan is a place for martial arts training; it is not for a social gathering. These activities are taken care of before or after class, preferably in the waiting area, NOT IN THE KUAN!

BOWS AND SALUTATIONS

Asian martial arts show respect with a Salutation. A salutation could be as simple as a slight bow at the waist or complex as a multiple move training form. Teachers, training halls, classmates, and martial artists from different systems are among the things we respect. Regardless of the reason, there is valuable training involved. There is no religious aspect to a martial art salutation.

SALUTATION HISTORY

Showing respect and bowing have been part of Chinese culture since K'ung Fu-Tzu [WG] (Confucius, 551 - 479 BC). The most widely used salute in Chinese martial arts is the wrapped fist [Pao-Ch'üan [WG] 包拳] (figure 2). In modern times we use Pao-Ch'üan when we greet someone, similar to a handshake in the west.

Figure 2

Ming loyalists, secret societies, and southern Shaolin arts used different versions of Pao-Ch'üan as a patriotic gesture during the Ch'ing dynasty (1644 - 1912). This has become a tradition in most Chinese martial arts. Some newer methods based on Chinese arts, such as Okinawan, Hawaiian, and American kempo/kenpo, also use variations of Pao-Ch'üan.

Historically, scholars wrapped their right hand around their left fist. However, military men and martial artists usually carried their weapons in their right hand, making it unsafe and inconvenient to perform the Pao-Ch'üan. This led to military men and martial artists wrapping their left hand around their right fist (whether they had a weapon or not).

During the Ch'ing Dynasty, Pao-Ch'üan was used as a patriotic gesture. The fist represents the character for Jih [WG] [Sun 日] (figure 3), and the open palm represents the character for Yueh [WG] [Moon 月] (figure 4). When combined, these two characters create the word Ming [WG] [Bright 明] (figure 5). People using a version of the Pao-Ch'üan salute essentially identified themselves as supporters of restoring the Ming to power.

Figure 3   Figure 4

The Pao-Ch'üan is also referred to in an old Hung-Men [WG] [red door or heroic society 紅門] initiation poem. *Green Dragon on my left, White Tiger on my right, I enter the Red Door.* The open left hand represents the Dragon; the right fist is the Tiger.

Figure 5

Today this handshape is called the "Warrior and Scholar" salute (figure 6). In this definition, the fist represents the warrior, and the palm represents the scholar. In line with this explanation, some schools say that the fist represents martial usage and the hand covering the fist shows civility. This definition is adhered to by many of today's Chinese martial arts practitioners.

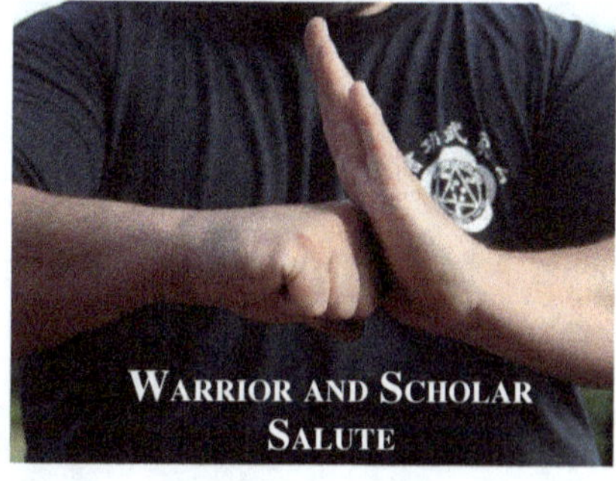

Figure 6

The definition espoused by the Peoples Republic of China states that the right fist means that you are pledged to the cultivation of the martial arts; the bent thumb of the left hand represents humility. The four extended fingers of the left hand symbolize uniting wu-shu across the four seas.

Martial Etiquette

There are many different versions of this basic hand gesture that various martial arts groups use; Each with unique characteristics and additional meanings. One of the more popular is when one stacked an open palm on top of a closed fist, this is known as Ng Wu Sei Hoi [CAN] or Wu-Hu Ssu-Hai [WG] [五湖四海] (figure 7). The meaning is, "Within the 5 lakes (Wu-Hu, the palm) and the 4 seas [Ssu-Hai, the fist], we are all brothers."

Figure 7

Salutations have evolved and changed with each generation. Once the Ch'ing Dynasty ended (1911), salutations became an identifying trademark of an individual martial system. An excellent example of this would be the Hung-Gar [CAN] [Hung-Chia [WG]] system. Hung-Gar has evolved into several different branches that are taught all over the world.

Figure 8

The original salute of Hung-Gar has the right fist alongside a left palm (figure 8); this is still used in some schools of Hung-Gar, most notable being schools in the Tang-Fung [CAN] (1879-1955) lineage. Some Hung-Gar schools make the left palm a tiger claw (figure 9), which was done after the death of Lam Sai-Wing [CAN] (1860-1943) by his students to distinguish his school from the other Hung-Gar schools. Lam Sai-Wing's school was called Hung-Kuen Fu-Hok Pai [CAN] [Hung's Fist, Tiger Crane School]; that's where the name "tiger and crane style" was first used. It does not represent all Hung-Gar lineages.

Figure 9

Another hand position that is sometimes seen is when both palms are pressed together in a prayer-like shape. This salute can be seen in systems that originated in India and Tibet. It is based on the Anjali mudra from India, where it is a gesture of greeting and reverence. It is the primary way to greet someone in both India and Tibet. There are different names for this, depending on the lineage represented. Hu-Chang [WG] [Greeting Palm合掌] (figure 10) is a term

Figure 10

used by some northern Shaolin methods; it is also called Buddhist palm by many martial systems. This salute is used in Northern Shaolin, La-Ma Pai [CAN], Bok-Hok Pai [CAN], Hop-Ga Pai [CAN], and Shorin-Ji Kempo [JAP].

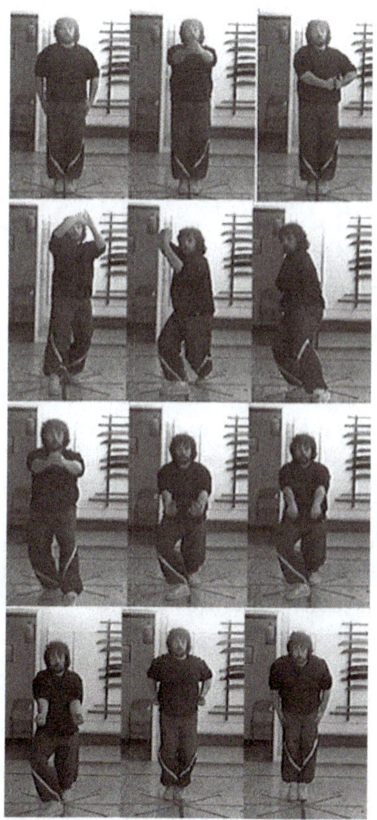

Figure 11

CEREMONIAL SALUTATION

Formal salutations, also known as Ceremonial bows [I-Shih Chu-Kung [WG],儀式鞠躬] are short forms or routines that are used for formal occasions (figure 11). These salutations were style and system-specific; they identify what martial system or school a practitioner represents. We use these salutations when we start or end training sessions and training routines or show respect to the school shrine. Many of these "ceremonial" salutations begin with two steps forward, followed by a Pao-Ch'üan. There are also times when a Pao-Ch'üan is issued in three directions (left, front and right) representing a triangle, symbolic of the three powers or San T'sai.

Ceremonial bows often start with your hands on the left side of the torso sweeping from left to right with a torso rotation, followed by the hands issuing the salute forward. The hands sweeping from one side to the other may have initially represented sweeping the Manchu [Ch'ing rulers] out of China. The Pao-Ch'uan moving left, right, and center may have initially represented the three powers [San T'sai]. In modern times this also shows respect to the past, present, and future teachers.

THE FIVE PRIMARY TYPES OF SALUTATION ARE:

Pao-Ch'üan: [Baoquan PY, 包拳] - Wrap (the) fist.

Hu-Chang: [Huzhang PY, 合掌] - Greeting palm.

Chu-Kung: [Jugong PY, 鞠躬] - Bow the head; bend at the waist. This term basically defines a standard bow that one might see in Japanese martial arts.

Ti-Tou: [Ditou PY, 低頭] - Dip the head. Essentially a lesser form of Chu-Kung.

I-Shih Chu-Kung: [Yishi Jugong PY, 儀式鞠躬] - A term describing what we in Pai-Lum call the ceremonial bow. It is made up of four words. The first two, I and Shih, when used together, mean ceremony. The next two, Chu and Kung, combine to mean bow.

WHAT WE SALUTE

The three primary things we salute in our martial training are teachers (past and present), training halls (training space and school shrine), and fists (style, system, forms). Chinese terms for these are:

Ching-Shih: [Jingshi PY, 敬師] - Respect the teacher.

Ching-Kuan: [Jingguan PY, 敬館] - Respect the training hall.

Ching-Ch'üan: [Jingquan PY, 敬拳] - Literally, respect (the) fist, in this case, fist, is used for paying respect to a style, system, art or form.

Issuing commands to salute

When teaching or leading a class, one issues a command for the students to salute. Pao-Ch'üan, Hu-Chang, Chu-Kung, Ti-T'ou, and I-Shih Chu-Kung are NOT commands to salute; they are descriptions of salutes. When one needs to issue a command to perform a salutation (for jr. classmates or students to pay respect to someone or something), the command that should be used is Hsing-Li.

> **Hsing-Li:** [Xingli [PY], 行禮] is the command to perform a salutation. In a Chinese grammatical form, it is called a verb-object, literally "salute [a] salute." A verb-object is often split apart with modifiers placed in between. For example, these modifiers can direct what kind of salute to perform, as in Hsing Ching-Kuan Li (do respect the training hall salute), or how to do the salute , as in Hsing Pao-Ch'üan Ti-T'ou Li (perform a salute wherein you place fist in the palm and nod the head).

> **Ging-Lai** [CAN] : [Ching-Li [WG], 敬禮]. Ging-Lai is a popular Cantonese term for salute. It is pronounced Jing-Li in the Mandarin dialect and essentially means respectful salute.

Pai family usage

Break stance

In Pai-Chia Ch'üan, we use a basic version of pao-ch'üan in our "break stance." In addition to showing respect, it is also used as an "attention" stance in class situations.

Description of a break stance

Feet are placed together, knees are slightly bent, the hips are curled forward, back is straight, eyes focused straight ahead, and the hands come together in pao-ch'üan just below the solar plexus on the centerline. Hands continue to punch out together (forward) as in a vertical fist punch. When told to relax, the hands are lowered, not dropped, to the sides. Break stance should be executed quickly, precisely as if striking someone directly in front of you. When executing a break stance, one should also exhale sharply from the tan-t'ien, creating the sound "soot."

Order of Break, when and how to use it:

1. The first person to see an Instructor enter or leave the training hall must call the class to break stance. This is done by yelling "break" or "li-jeng."

Exceptions:

a. The Instructor in question waves the class off, indicating that he/she will be in and out and does not wish to interrupt training.

b. The Instructor in question is of lower rank than another instructor already on the training floor.

2. Any time a junior student comes in contact with an Instructor. On or off the training floor (unless waved off).

3. Any time a junior student wishes to ask an Instructor a question.

4. Any time a student has business with a training hall manager, owner, or Instructor in the office. He/she will come to the doorway of the office and stand in a break stance until recognized.

5. Any time a student wishes to leave a class for any reason other than they are going to be physically sick.

Other things to note about break stance.

1. Do not move while in break stance unless told to by the Instructor.

2. When leaving an Instructor, come to a break stance and back up three paces before turning.

*** Never turn your back on an Instructor ***

ENTERING & EXITING THE KUAN

Although kuan usually refers to the entire space, the training area is considered special. It is usually separated by either a doorway or a line on the floor. Only students and instructors are allowed in this area.

Upon entering a kuan, a student should perform your school's salutation or bow (usually towards the shrine) and enter the training area. This is done to respect the past, present, and future masters of the art (or arts) taught at the kuan. This also symbolizes you are leaving your everyday life outside of the training area so that you may concentrate on the training.

The salutations which the Pai Family system uses to pay respect to the kuan serve many purposes. For martial reasons, the student is made to move in a specific way so that they are training the following skills:

1. moving from the hips

2. bending the knees

3. curling the hips

4. pivoting

5. cat stance

6. awareness

7. forward mental pressure

When entering the training area, step up to the line (a line on the floor that determines where the actual training area begins) with the right foot (toe-out 45 degrees; figure 12). Step across the line with the left foot into a left cat stance (figures 13-14) and execute the pao-ch'üan salute (elbows slightly bent, wrists are straight, hips are curled, and the knees are bent). Place hands at sides and continue onto the training floor.

ENTERING SALUTE (LONG VERSION)

The long salute is done the first time entering a training area during the day and the last time leaving the training area on the same day. This salute pays respect to the kuan and the past, present, and future masters. After performing the short salute raise your hands to a position forward and somewhat higher than your forehead, palms facing outward (right hand in a fist with the left hand backing it up). Pivot on the heel of the right foot, so you are facing 45 degrees to the left. Maintaining the same stance and hand position, pivot 90 degrees to the right. Pivot to the front (towards the center of the kuan), bring the hands back down to the pao-ch'üan posture, and continue to enter or exit the kuan. Both the left foot and the right toes travel in an arc while pivoting on the right heel. Please note that both feet turn at the same time.

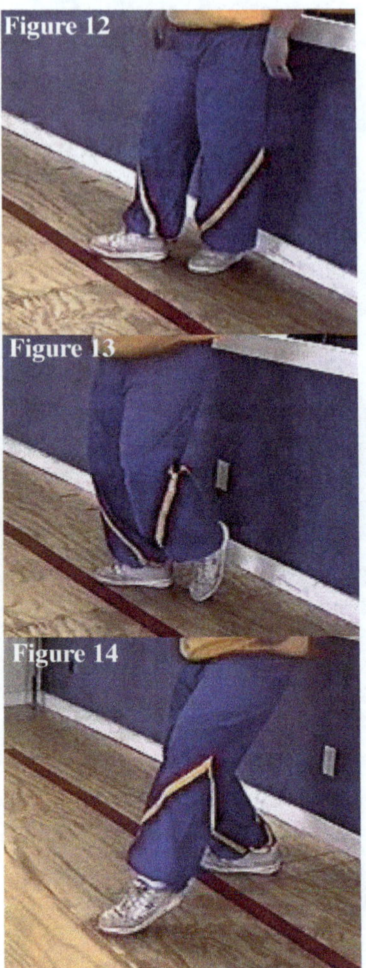

When exiting, step up to the line with the left foot (figure 15-16), step out of the kuan with right foot (toe up, no weight on foot; figure 17), turn whole body 90 degrees to the left (until pigeon-toed; figure 18), shift all weight on the right foot, pull hands up into chamber position as the left heel is raised (figure 19). Turn waist to the left (by moving R. hip towards training area) while placing left foot in cat stance position (facing back into the kuan; figure 20) and finish salute. If possible, back out at least three steps (placing hands at sides) before turning away from the training floor.

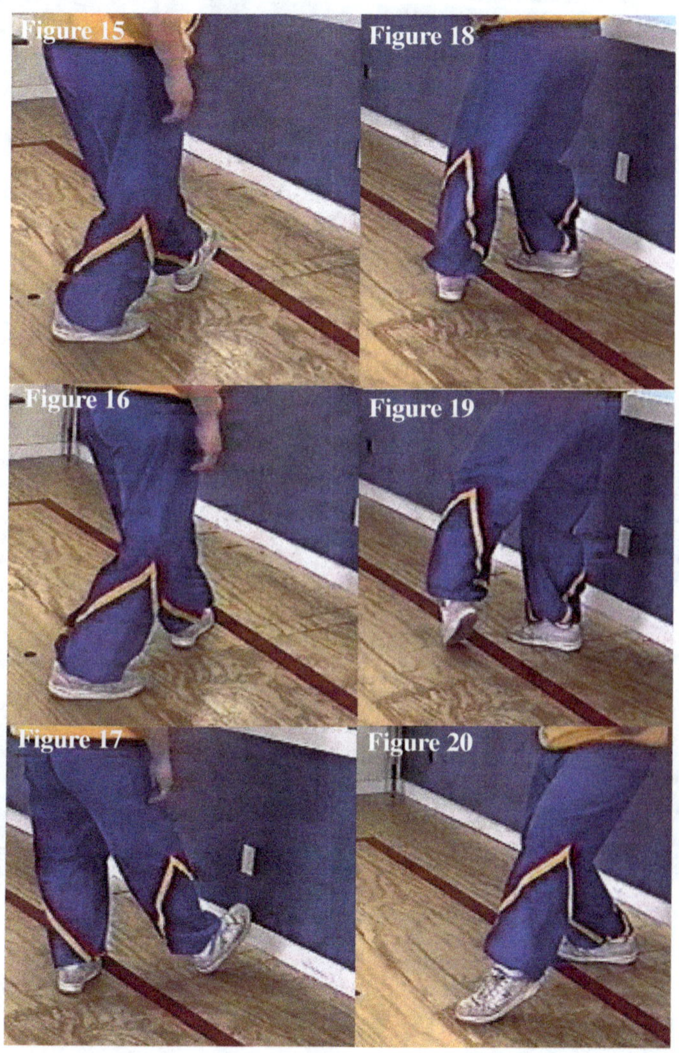

     Martial Etiquette

Grandmaster Daniel K. Pai leading class in Florida, 1974

- Photo by James Wilson

Chapter Four

IV THE ART

THREE STAGES OF MARTIAL TRAINING

There are three stages of martial training; Fundamentals, Forms, and Usage; sometimes written as Fundamentals, Forms, and Function; the three Fs (in Japanese, it would be Kihon, Kata, and Kumite; the three Ks). Throughout your martial career, you will constantly be going through these stages.

Fundamentals [Chi-Ben Kung 基本功] are the foundation upon which the entire art is based. Structural shapes, stance work, striking, kicking, breathing, core principles, strength training, endurance training, etc. ALL martial art training uses these building blocks.

Forms [Lien Ch'üan-Tao 練拳套] are the linking together of fundamentals for refining and practicing your art. These linked form sequences are two or more techniques put together in a particular way for practice, memorization, and future learning. Two-person forms are any pre-arranged or choreographed drill or form sequence practiced interactively with another person.

Functionality is proper usage. Usage [Yung Fa 用法] is any practice, application, and use of martial skills against another person. Technique application, two-person practice, sparring, and self-defense are examples of usage.

Principles, Concepts, and Theories

In the context we are using here, principles are rules or laws governing how the human body moves. Martial principles, or principles used in martial arts, are rules or laws of movement associated with martial training.

Martial concepts and theories are the ideas and practices of using and combining martial principles for specific purposes.

Every martial art practitioner, system, and style uses the same principles in practice and application. When, how, or why we use these principles are determined by martial theory, level of understanding, and stylistic preference. For example, the principle of push is the same in every martial art. How and in what circumstances push is used is based on experience, conceptual understanding, usage theory, stylistic preference, or simply when needed.

Our training begins with learning how to move (structure, alignment, articulation), create force (striking, kicking, blocking, breathing), issue force (target selection, distance, timing), and absorb and dissipate force (yielding, springy energy).

Fundamentals are designed to facilitate this learning. They are generally practiced in a large, exaggerated way to allow you to feel what you are doing and make adjustments before creating bad habits that hinder your progress. With constant drilling and proper practice, you will internalize these skills; they will become your natural movements.

Principle of Force:

Force equals mass times acceleration ($F=MxA$); this is the equation for force.

When we begin training, we focus on the ability to create force in our basic techniques. The principle of force is used whenever you are blocking, striking, or kicking something. Two of the biggest problems in creating force are friction in movement and the inability to maximize the percentage of our usable mass. The force we create is initiated with a pushing or pulling action.

Force can be increased by:

Increasing the rate of acceleration

Adding more usable mass

Reducing friction

There are many types of force, and how to issue force into a target involved in martial training.   As the student's skills evolve, they will be exposed to many of them.

Principle of the heel and hip:

Proper hip structure, alignment, and articulation are essential for the proper energy transfer from the legs to the upper body.

It is essential in creating and issuing force that the striking side of the body moves toward the target. When the striking side hip moves toward the target, the thigh, toes, and heel also move toward the target, allowing for mass movement. When the heel moves away from the target, the hip's forward movement, at best, is minimized. Often, the hip will not move toward the target; in many cases, it will move away. This results in less mass being available to create force.

Initially, the three primary things we need to know about the hip and heel are:

Where the heel goes, the hip goes.

Where the heel refuses to go, the hip is blocked from going.

The foot is the analog of the hip:

The heel matches the butt cheek (gluteus maximus).

The toe matches the point of the hip, or ASIS (anterior superior iliac spine).

Principle of Forward:

Forward is defined as the direction of our opponent in relation to any part of our anatomy. Toward the enemy's center is forward:

The hips curl forward (primarily on the striking or issuing side).
When moving forward, do so with forward pressure. ("ch'i" and "i")

When moving to the side, do so with forward pressure.

When moving backward, do so with forward pressure.

PRINCIPLE OF PUSH:

A push is an exertion of force that moves away from the source of that force. Pushing, shoving, bumping, and thrusting (strikes and kicks) fit this category.

PRINCIPLE OF PULL:

A pull is an exertion of force that moves toward the source of that force. Pulling, plucking, tugging, drawing, tearing, and rending fit this category.

PRINCIPLE OF FULL AND EMPTY:

Full and empty define the weight or energy distribution of the legs. The legs share 100% of the body's weight. When 100% of the weight or energy is on one leg, it is considered full; when a leg has 0% percent of the weight or energy, it is considered empty. When a leg fills, it receives weight and energy from the opposite leg, which is simultaneously emptying; it is transferring or issuing energy to the filling side. A filling leg is pulling, and an emptying leg is pushing. This shifting of weight is the initial phase of creating force.

Push with the hand opposite the full or filling leg; fill the leg opposite the pushing hand.

Pull with the hand on the same side as the full or filling leg; fill the leg on the same side as the pulling hand.

Usually, the filling or receiving leg is bending, while the emptying or issuing leg is straightening.

The job of the leg on the same side as the pushing hand is to stay out of the way of that hip (reducing friction).

Empty does not mean insubstantial. Relaxed does not equal limp. Full does not mean rigid.

Anatomic and Movement Definitions

In the ordinary course of learning martial techniques, students mimic and emulate the movements shown to them by instructors and classmates. Details essential for efficiently using these techniques are acquired by learning and incorporated, through practice, into their training. When there is no instructor, clear and concise terminology is needed. The anatomic terminology in this manual is based on standard terminology that describes fundamental articulation, planes of movement, and directions of movement related to these planes. This terminology is used so that people can figure out how to properly articulate shapes and techniques when they do not have someone physically showing them.

Planes of Movement

We use three planes when describing where something is, or the direction something is moving concerning a human body: the Sagittal plane, Coronal plane, and Transverse plane:

Sagittal Plane - The Sagittal plane divides the body into right and left halves, also known as the mid-sagittal or median plane.

Coronal Plane - The coronal plane divides the body into a front (anterior) and back (posterior) half, also known as the frontal plane.

Transverse Plane - The Transverse plane separates the body into upper (superior) and lower (inferior) halves, also known as the horizontal plane.

Medial and Lateral

Medial and Lateral define how close to the Sagittal plane something is. Medial describes something closer to or moving toward the Sagittal plane. Lateral describes things that are farther away from or moving away from the Sagittal plane.

The pinky side is the medial or inside of the hand and forearm. The thumb side is the lateral or outside of the hand and forearm.

Ventral and Dorsal

Ventral (anterior) and Dorsal (posterior) describe the front or back of an organism. The palm side of the forearm is the front or ventral side, while the opposite is the back or dorsal side. The forearm's ventral or front of the forearm

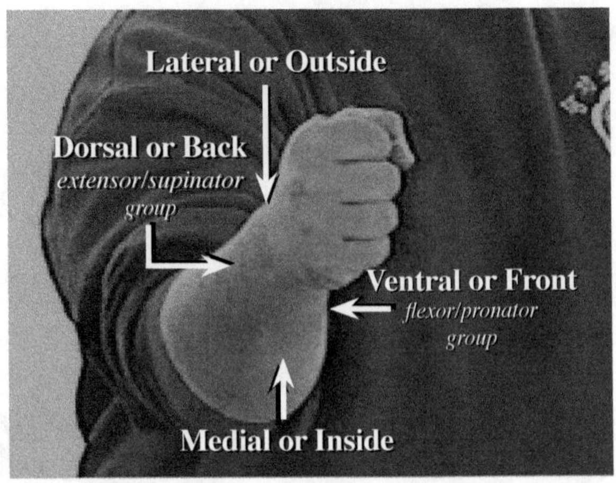

primarily contains the flexor/pronator muscles, while the dorsal or backside primarily contains the extensor/supinator muscles.

Adduction and Abduction

Moving a body part towards a mid-line reference point is Adduction. Moving a body part away from a mid-line reference point is Abduction.

Opening Arc, Closing Arc, Thrust, Pull, Step, and Breathe

Opening arc, closing arc, thrust, pull, step, and breath are simplified terms we use for the six actions that make up our art.

Opening Arc

Opening arc techniques are applied during the extension or opening of a limb; this can also be defined as increasing the angle of a joint. Strikes happen during the hinging extension of a limb or a lateral movement of an arm or leg, including the opening of the shoulders, hips, and waist rotation. Arching the back to strike backward with the head or buttocks are also considered opening arc skills. Opening arc movements are powered primarily by extensor (Yang) muscles; this is centrifugal force, and its effect is at right angles to the length of the striking limb.

CLOSING ARC

Closing arc techniques are applied during the flexion or closing of a limb; this can also be defined as decreasing the angle of a joint. Strikes happen during the hinging contraction or medial movement of an arm or leg, including the closing of the shoulders, hips, and waist rotation. Using abdominals to strike forward with the head, thigh, or shoulder is also considered a closing arc. Closing arc movements are powered primarily by flexor (Yin) muscles; this is centripetal force. Its effect is also at right angles to the length of the striking limb.

THRUST

Thrusting techniques are strikes that follow the principle of Push. The line of force is along the length of the striking limb from the structural center of the previous anatomical joint and the point of contact or striking surface.

PULL

Pulling is any technique that follows the principle of pull. When initiating a pulling action, the line of force is from the point of contact (grab or hook) along the length of the pulling limb through the structural center of the previous anatomic joint (elbow). Pulling actions are the opposite of thrusting actions. Ninety percent of all pulls turn into a sinking or pushing action.

STEP

Stepping is how we create energy from the legs, advance, evade, retreat, and kick. The definition of a kick is a step with a different dynamic. Any step that cannot become a kick is a poorly executed stepping skill. Opening arc, closing arc, and thrusting qualities are also found in kicking skills. Weight shifting, rooting, jumping, turning, spinning, and accelerating body mass are all created or facilitated by stepping. The term we use for stance is Pu, the Mandarin word for step; this implies that stance work must be alive and active, not un-moving like a statue.

The Art

BREATHE

Breathing supplies the body with oxygen; it is how we energize our body. Proper breathing helps with the execution of techniques. Breath training is Ch'i Kung [氣功]. Martial power is Chin [勁], Chin is a combination of physical strength [Li 力], breath [Ch'i 氣], and intent [I 意].

QUALITIES OF MARTIAL MOVEMENT

SHEN-SUO

Shen-Suo [伸縮] represents the expanding and contracting qualities associated with Dragon style movements. Shen: To extend, stretch out, open up. Suo: To withdraw, to pull back, to contract, to shrink, to reduce, to abbreviate.

T'AN-CHIN

T'an-chin [彈勁] means Elastic or Springy energy. When practicing or applying martial arts, your limbs and torso should have an elastic or springy quality. The two types of "Spring-like" qualities we use are compressive and extension, or tension. A compression spring becomes shorter under load; it resists compression. A tension or extension spring becomes longer under load; it resists stretching.

Any contact between your arms and an opponent's arms (such as blocking, striking, bridging, pushing hands, spinning hands, sensing hands, or sticky hands) requires your arms to have a springy or elastic quality for the following reasons:

If your arms are extended too far, you are vulnerable; you can easily be pulled off-balance, putting you in a compromised position, and defensively, your torso and limbs are open to attack. This situation requires the spring quality of tension or extension.

If your arms are too close to your body or your shoulders are pulled back too far, they will collapse if attacked. This situation requires the structural alignment of having the elbows bent at least 90 degrees and the shoulders being slightly forward of the spine. This structure allows for the use of compressive spring energy to absorb and deflect strikes.

SPIRALING [TSUAN 鑽]

The American Heritage Dictionary defines a spiral as "A three-dimensional curve that turns around an axis at a constant or continuously varying distance while moving parallel to the axis; a helix." Helical or spiral movement is an essential quality in most martial skills. Any twisting, winding, turning, coiling, wrapping, or rotating movement contains a spiral.

Ch'an Ssu Chin [纏絲勁 Silk Reeling Energy] is the most famous example of spiral energy training. The term Ch'an Ssu Chin was first used by Ch'en Hsin (1849-1929) in association with Ch'en Style T'ai-Chi Ch'üan. Ch'en Hsin was a famous T'ai-Chi Ch'üan theorist who wrote the classic text "Illustrated Explanations of Ch'en Family T'ai-Chi Ch'üan" in the 1920s.

Two obvious spiraling techniques of the arms are the full-twist punch practiced in most Kung-Fu, Kempo, and Karate systems and the drilling fist of Hsing-I Ch'üan. When articulating either of these techniques, the forearm's rotation, twisting, or rending actions are known as ulnar or radial deviation. Ulnar deviation or flexion is when the arm rotates to create a palm-facing downward position (pronation). Radial deviation or flexion is when the arm rotates to create a palm-facing upward position (supination).

Full-twist front punch is a spiraling action of the forearm created by ulnar flexion; rotating the forearm from a palm-up position to a palm-down position (the pinky side of the hand rotates laterally, and the thumb-side of the fist rotates medially). The hand ends in a palm-down position (pronation). Essentially, linking a palm-up, vertical, and palm-down punch together.

Drilling fist [Tsuan Ch'üan, 鑽拳] is a spiraling technique created by radial flexion; rotating the forearm from a palm-down position to a palm-up position (the pinky side of the hand rotates medially, and the thumb side rotates later-

55

ally). The hand ends in a palm-up position (supination). Essentially linking a palm-down, vertical, and palm-up punch together. This technique is also referred to as a reverse twist punch by some Pai-Lum practitioners.

Drilling is a core skill embedded in our fundamental blocking, bridging, and striking methods.

AXIS OF ROTATION

In this section, we will illustrate how a technique is changed by using a different axis of rotation. Slightly changing the axis of rotation has a major effect on any technique. Understanding this allows us to adjust our techniques to be more efficient and adaptable to any situation. Awareness of the various axes of rotation in one's stance work, kicking, and striking skills, and our opponent's axes of rotation for grappling and throwing techniques, is of the utmost importance if we want to elevate the quality of our art.

While there are many potential axes of rotation, we focus on three when learning this concept applied to thrusting-type hand techniques. The first axis is from the center of the elbow through the middle finger; the pinky and thumb rotate equally around this axis. The second axis is from the center of the elbow through the thumb; the hand rotates around this axis. The third axis is from the center of the elbow through the pinky; the hand rotates around this axis.

Example A is a Palm Strike [Chang Ta, 掌打] from a palm-up position. In this technique, there are three examples of applying a different axis of rotation to the technique. In example A, the action consists of going from a palm up to a palm down position (pronation). The axis is shown as a white line from the elbow through the hand. The arrows show the direction of the energy. (This is the same general articulation as a full twist front punch using a palm to illustrate the movements better)

Example B is a Drilling Fist [Tsuan Ch'üan, 鑽拳] (AKA reverse twist punch or upset punch) from a palm down position. In this technique, there are three examples of applying a different axis of rotation to the technique. In example B, the action consists of going from a palm-down to a palm-up position (supination).

The axis is shown as a white line from the elbow through the hand. The arrows show the direction of the energy in each example.

EXAMPLE A

This example illustrates how slight variations in the axis of rotation of the forearm can affect the outcome and functionality of a basic palm strike.

Version one (figure 21): The axis of rotation is from the center of the elbow through the middle finger's knuckle. Both the thumb and pinky rotate around the axis equally. This technique is a basic forward thrust with the rotation of the arm, adding another point of acceleration.

Figure 21

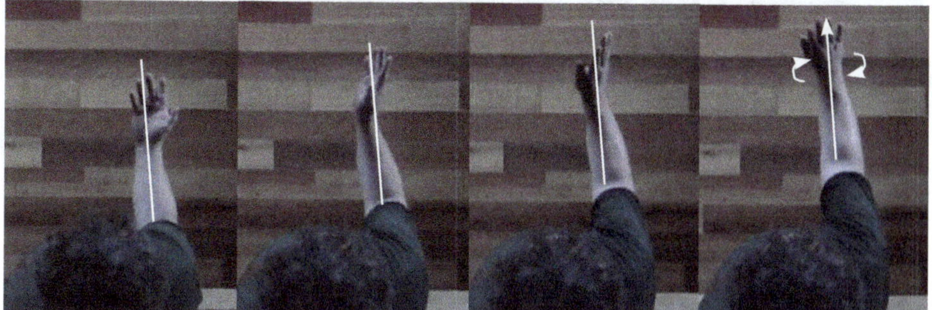

Version two (figure 22): The axis of rotation is from the center of the elbow through the knuckle of the pinky. The thumb and center of the palm rotate around the axis. This technique is a forward thrust with the rotation of the arm, creating an inward palm strike.

Figure 22

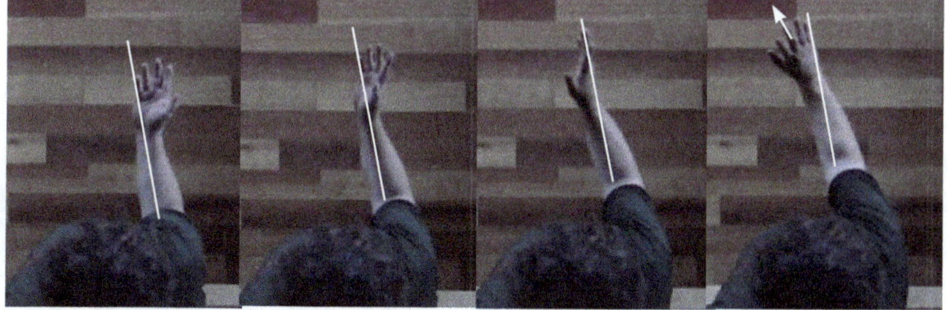

The Art

Version three (figure 23): The axis of rotation is from the center of the elbow through the index finger's knuckle. The edge and center of the palm rotate around the axis. This technique is a forward thrust with the rotation of the arm, creating a forward and slightly outward palm/knife edge strike.

Figure 23

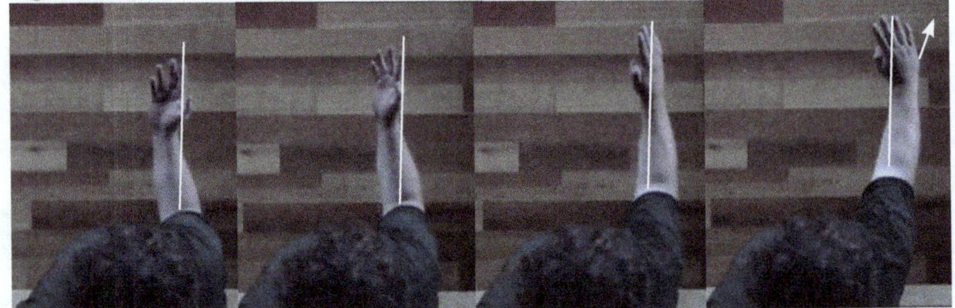

EXAMPLE B

This example illustrates how slight variations in the axis of rotation of the forearm can affect the outcome and functionality of a drilling punch.

Version one (figure 24): The axis of rotation is from the center of the elbow through the middle finger's knuckle. Both the thumb and pinky rotate around the axis equally. This technique is a basic forward punch with the rotation of the arm, adding another point of acceleration.

Figure 24

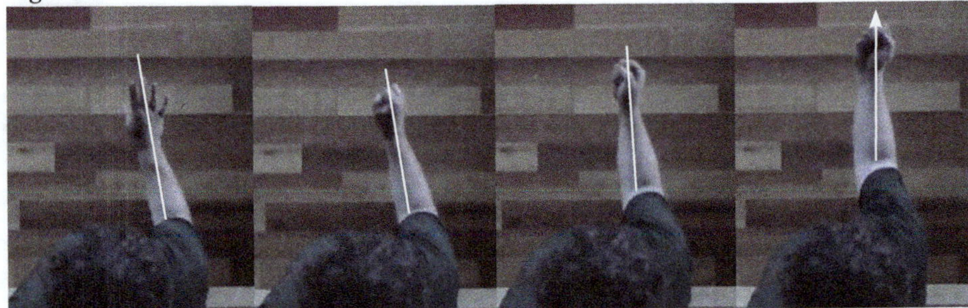

Version two (figure 25): The axis of rotation is from the center of the elbow through the index finger's knuckle. The pinky and center of the palm rotate around the axis. This technique is a forward drill with the rotation of the arm, creating an inward blocking action with the forearm and an inward hammer fist.

Figure 25

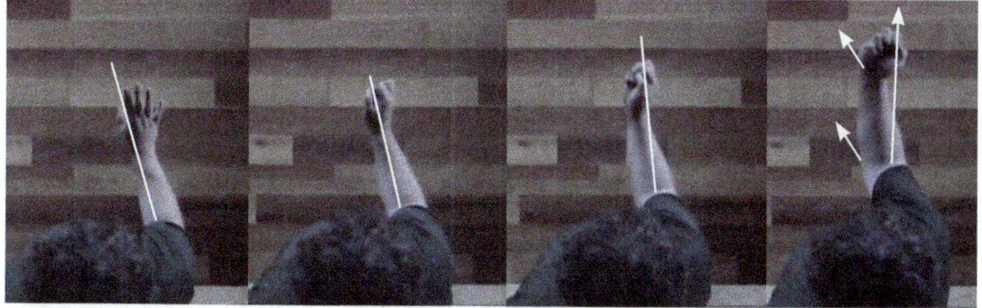

Version three (figure 26): The axis of rotation is from the center of the elbow through the pinky. The back of the index finger's first knuckle and the center of the palm rotates around the axis. This technique is a forward and slightly outward thrust with the rotation of the arm creating a forward and slightly outward drilling action. Rotating around this axis creates an outward blocking action and back knuckle.

Figure 26

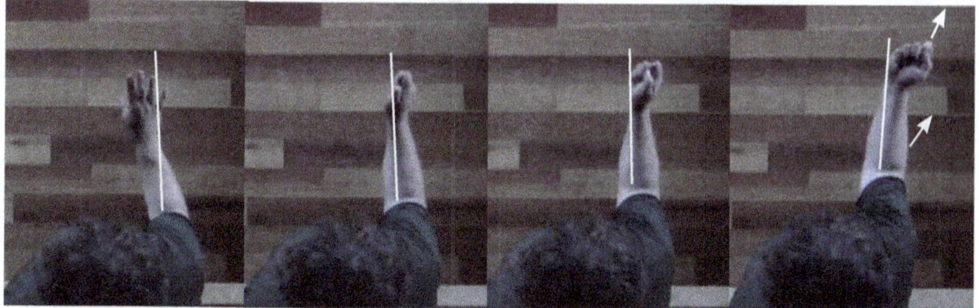

The Art

Daniel K. Pai breaking ice at Wickham park, Manchester, CT.
This was taken during a photoshoot for the
"Masters' World of Kung-Fu and Karate" demonstrations.
- Photo by David Everett

Chapter Five

V FUNDAMENTAL SHAPES
Hand Shapes, Foot Shapes, Stances

Fundamental Shapes   [Chi-Ben Hsing 基本形]

Like any other endeavor, a strong, structurally correct foundation is required if you plan to take your art past the novice level of ability or understanding. Fundamental training is more than just the physical; it also introduces the principles and concepts that all martial arts are built upon.

In Chinese martial arts, the word for shape or form is Hsing [形]. To perform and apply any of the skills in the four areas of martial development, you need to know fundamental shapes and how to apply them. These shapes are the raw materials you need to build a solid foundation for your training. By shapes, we mean what positions different parts of your body have to be in during a fundamental action like punching or kicking. For example, to kick, you have to be stable on one side of your body while allowing your opposite leg to be articulated in such a way to facilitate striking something with a part of your foot/leg that can be used as a weapon. All of these "shapes" are reference points and teaching tools for learning the art. Here are the shapes and techniques (which are multiple shapes put together for a specific purpose) that we consider our fundamentals:

Hand shapes [Shou Hsing 手形]

When we talk about shapes and forms, we are talking about what something looks like. In most cases, this requires specific structural qualities such as skeletal alignment. Many hand shapes are used in martial arts; they are used for striking, grabbing, pushing, pulling, or hooking. Hand shapes are divided into two groups; closed hand or open hand. Initial training usually focuses on closed hand or fist shapes. Figure 27 illustrates how to form a basic fist.

Figure 27

BASIC FIST FORMATION

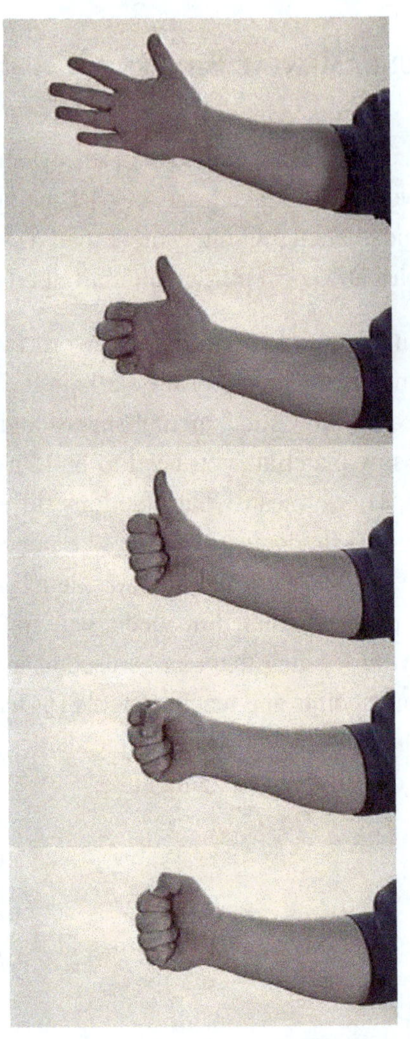

1. Start with the hand open.

2. Keeping the thumb straight, bend the fingers at the 3rd and 2nd knuckle.

3. Continue bending the fingers at the 1st set of knuckles.

4. Wrap the thumb around the index and middle fingers.

5. Place the thumb on top of the index finger as an alternate way to hold the thumb.

FIST [CH'ÜAN 拳]

AKA Quan [PY], Kuen [CAN], Ken [JAP].

A fist is a hand shape or form in which the fingers are closed into the palm, with the thumb pressed down, wrapping the index and middle finger, or held tight to the ridge of the hand with the thumb pressing down on the index finger.

There are many striking surfaces on a fist, as well as several different fist types. While not as versatile as an open hand, the fist is the primary weapon in most martial methods.

Figure 28 illustrates the striking surfaces of the fist and the area of the fist face used for basic punching techniques.

Figure 28

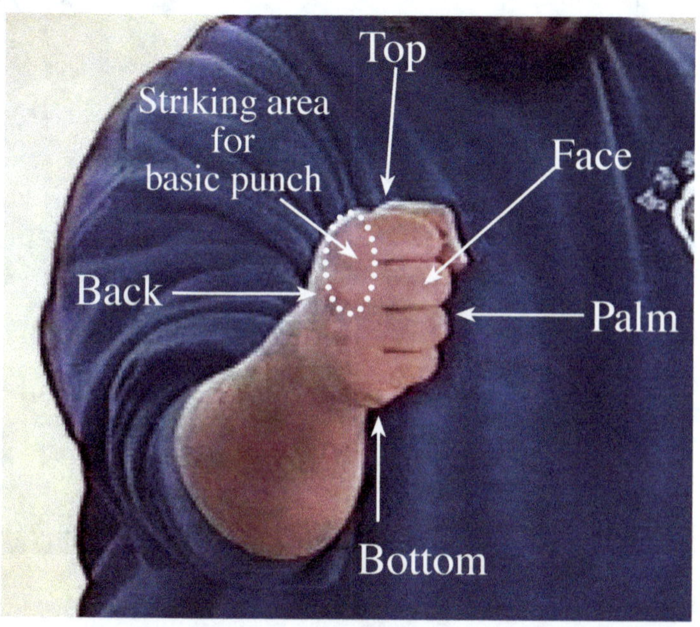

The primary use of the fist is punching (using the fist in a thrusting manner). The contact area, when punching, is the 1st knuckles of the index and middle finger. This structure is used in snapping, point penetration, and thrusting punches. The fist can be oriented in any direction when punching (palm up, palm in, palm down, palm out, and anywhere in between).

A fist with the palm facing upward [Chang Shang Ch'üan 掌上拳] is used for straight punches, uppercuts, and drilling fists.

A palm inward fist position is called a vertical or standing fist [Li Ch'üan 立拳], it is also known as sun fist [Jih Ch'üan 日拳] because it resembles the Chinese character for sun.

A palm facing down fist is called a horizontal or flat fist [P'ing Ch'üan 平拳].

The classical punching action, known as full twist punch, is a combination of palm up, vertical, and horizontal punches linked together in one smooth technique (figure 29 and 30). Note the 3/4 twist fist position in figure 29; it is often used in Southern Chinese and Okinawan methods.

Fists are also used in opening arc and closing arc striking. These strikes will use all parts of the fist.

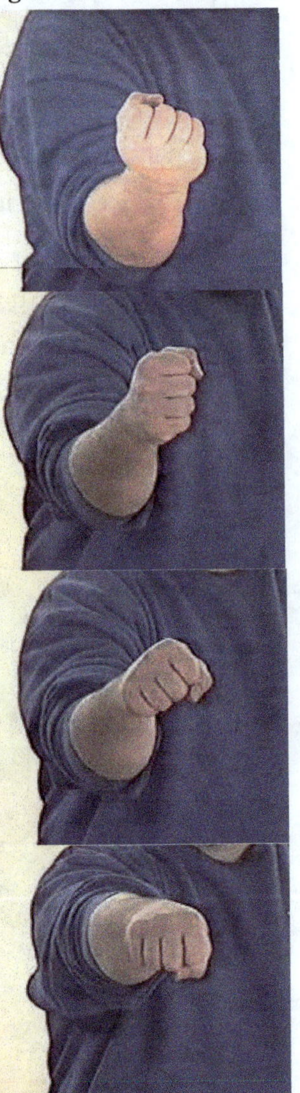

Figure 29

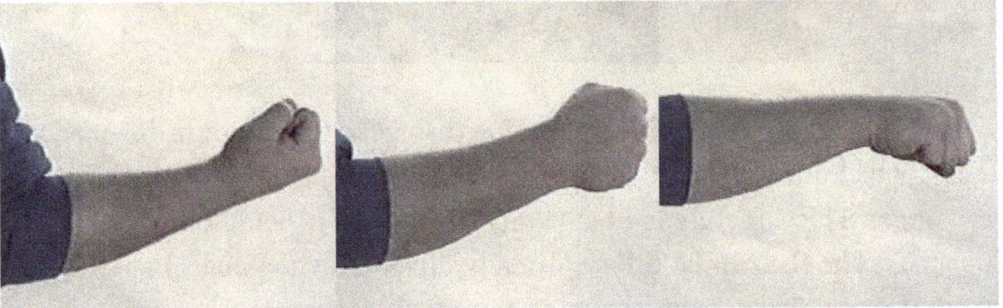

Figure 30

Hammer fist [ch'ui ch'üan 捶拳]

AKA Ken Tsui [JAP] (Hammer Fist), Ch'ui Shou [WG] (Hammer hand),

Shu Tsui [JAP] (Hammer Hand)

The hammer fist, or inverted hammer fist, is a shape that uses the bottom or top of the fist respectively. The hammer fist is used in opening arc strikes; the inverted hammer fist is used in closing arc strikes. Figure 30 shows the striking surface used for hammer fist and inverted hammer fist techniques.

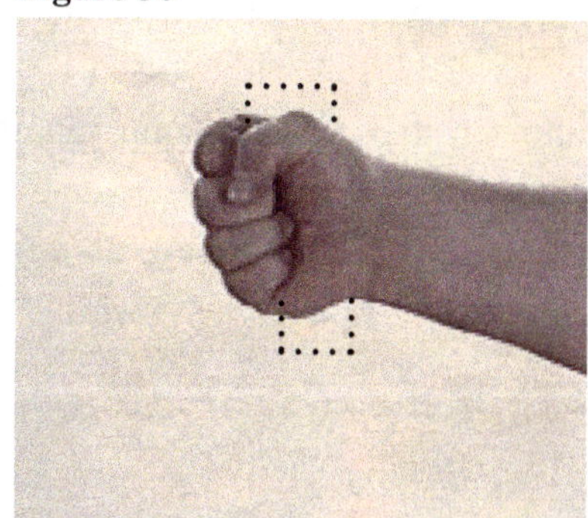

Figure 30

Back fist [pei ch'üan 背拳]

AKA Ura-Ken [JAP] (Back of Fist)

The back fist, or back knuckle, is used in opening arc strikes and is a very common use of the fist. Used in essentially the same way, back fist strikes issue energy to a fairly large surface area, while back knuckle strikes affect a smaller area and penetrate deeper into the target.

Figure 31 shows the striking surface used for back fist. Figure 32 shows the striking surface for back knuckle strikes.

Figure 31

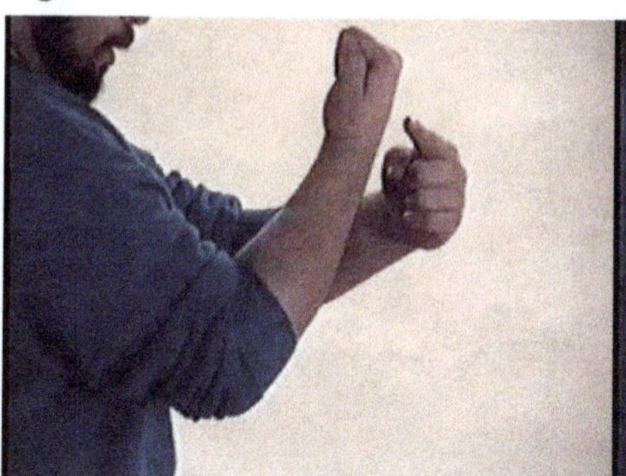

Figure 32

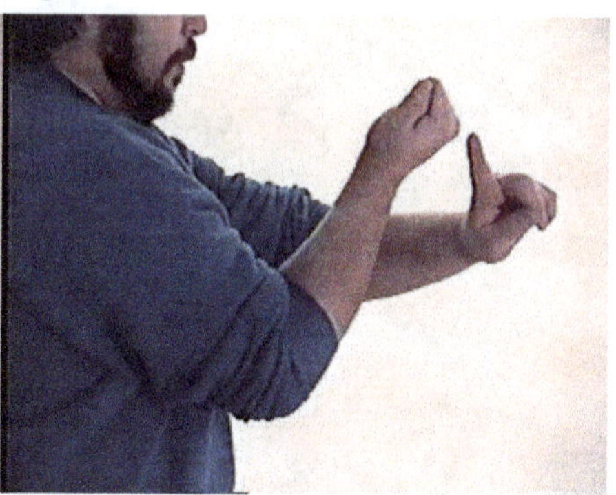

Fundamental Shapes

AKA Ginger Fist, Ippon-Ken [JAP] (single knuckle fist), Sho-Ken [JAP] (one knuckle fist)

The phoenix eye fist is a basic fist with the index finger extended to the second knuckle. A widely used weapon, the phoenix eye fist punches or grinds into sensitive areas.   Feng yan ch'üan is the primary fist of Pai-Mei Ch'üan (Pak Mei Kuen) and some schools of Southern Praying Mantis. Figure 33 shows the striking surface used for the phoenix eye fist.

Figure 33

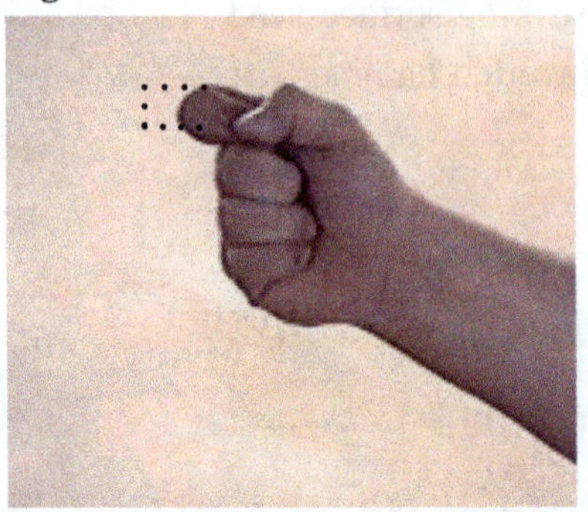

DRAGON HEAD FIST [LUNG T'OU CH'ÜAN 龍頭拳]

AKA Ippon-Ken [JAP] (single knuckle fist)

The dragon head fist is a basic fist with the middle finger extended to the second knuckle. The dragon head fist is used in punching or closing arc strikes. Figure 34 shows the striking surface used for the dragon head fist.

Figure 34

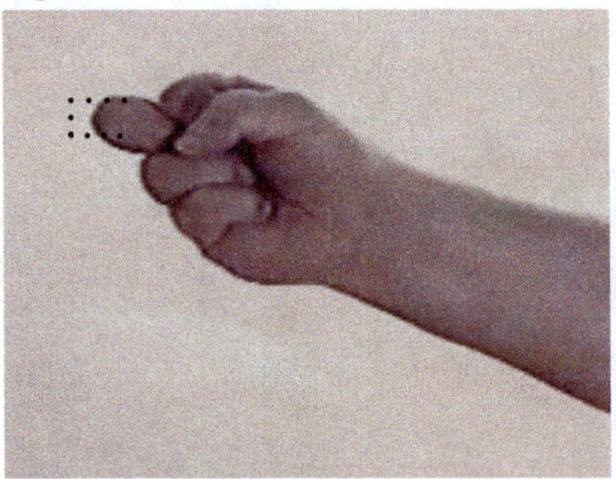

Leopard fist [Pao ch'üan 豹拳]

AKA Hira-Ken [JAP] (fore-knuckle fist)

The leopard fist is a flattened fist extended to the second knuckle, AKA Ch'üan Feng [拳峰 peak of the fist]. This fist is very thin and can fit into tight spaces, like the neck. It is also used in closing arc strikes, raking the knuckles across the opponent. Figure 35 shows the striking surface used for the leopard fist.

Figure 35

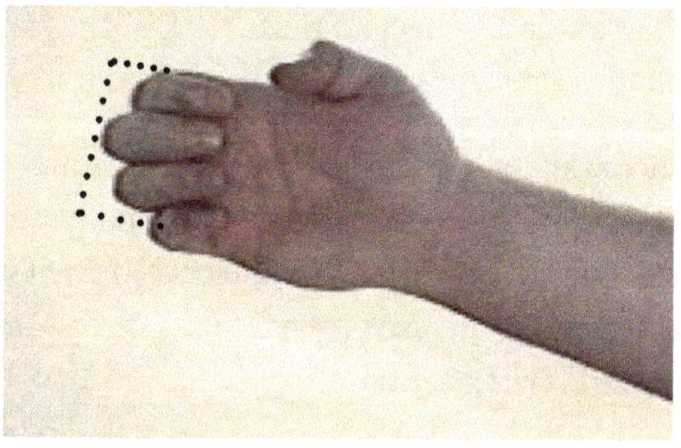

Crane head fist [He t'ou ch'üan 鶴頭拳]

AKA Ch'üan Feng [拳峰 peak of the fist]

The crane head fist is a basic fist shape with the thumb pressing against the side of the index finger. This fist strikes with the second set of knuckles. One of the ways to apply this fist is to strike as if knocking on a door. In addition, it may be used in several raking actions. The crane head and dragon head fists may be used similarly, except the crane head fist will strike a larger area. This fist works very well against the side of the head, nose, chest, arms, and back of the hand. Figure 36 shows the striking area of the crane head fist.

Figure 36

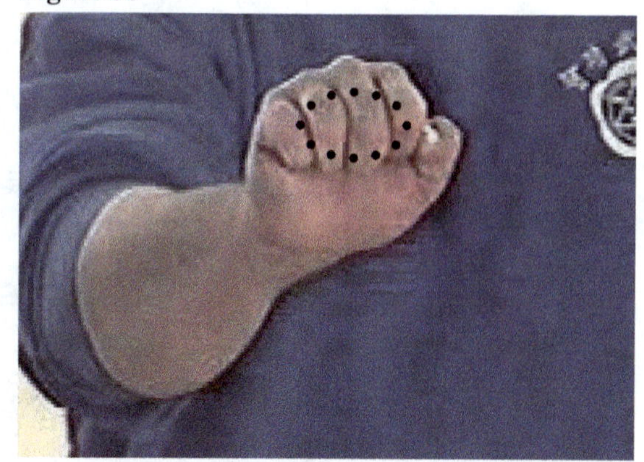

The open hand is a much more diverse weapon than the fist. It is used to attack body parts that fist shapes don't fit into or cannot reach, manipulate an opponent's limbs, and grab/grasp an opponent. While some open-hand shapes are explicitly used for striking, there is always the potential for clawing, hooking, or grabbing after the strike. In Pai Family Martial Arts, this is the standard, not the exception. Grabbing, clawing, and hooking are done in concert with the forearms in most parry/blocking skills. Many claws (when used to grab and manipulate an opponent) and most hook shapes are employed after initial contact with the opponent with one's hands and forearms.

In this section, arrows (◄———), if they are pointing towards a hand, will be used to show a specific part of the hand. If it is pointing away from a hand, it will show the line of force of a strike. A single curved line (⌣) will show what parts of a hand position are used for hooking. Three curved lines (≋) will show grabbing or clawing actions.

The parts of the open hand used in martial arts are shown in figure 37. In general, when using the open hand for striking, the thumb is usually held tightly against the ridge of the hand in a similar fashion to the fist. The exceptions are when one strikes with the ridge, back of the wrist or when applying pecking techniques.

Figure 37

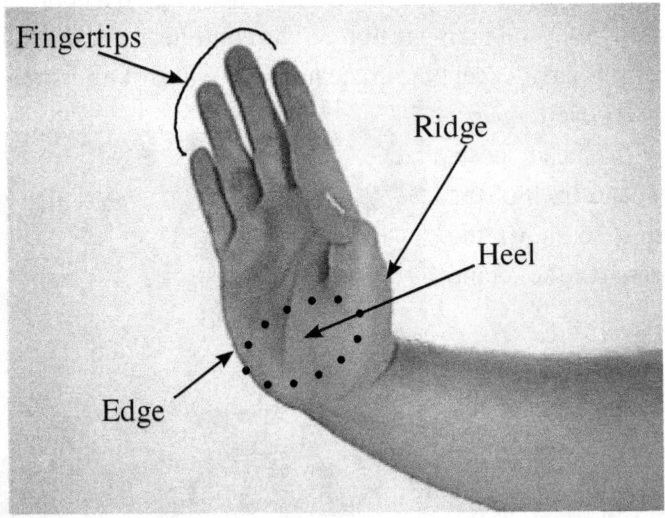

When using the empty hand as a weapon, there are some general rules that are pretty much the same in all systems.

1. Any strike using the fingertips in a thrusting manner is a spear hand.

2. Any strike using the edge of the palm is considered a knife hand.

3. Any strike using the ridge of the hand is considered a ridge hand strike.

4. Any strike using the palm is considered a palm strike.

5. Any strike using the backside of the hand is considered a backhand.

6. Any strike using the back of the wrist is considered a wrist strike.

7. Any strike using the fingertips bunched together is considered pecking.

8. Any time the fingers flex to create a clawing action or a grab, it is considered a claw.

9. Any time the wrist is bent to form a sharp angle between the hand and the arm, it is considered a hook.

PALM [CHANG 掌]

The palm shape in figure 38 is called Standing Palm [Li-Chang 立掌]. AKA: Teisho [JAP] (Palm Heel).

The palm is used to strike an opponent in many ways. One of the primary uses is a thrusting technique, striking with the heel of the palm. Many opening and closing arc strikes utilize the palm (such as slapping and clawing techniques). Iron Palm, Vibrating Palm, and Suction Palm are very famous techniques that utilize the palm.

Figure 38

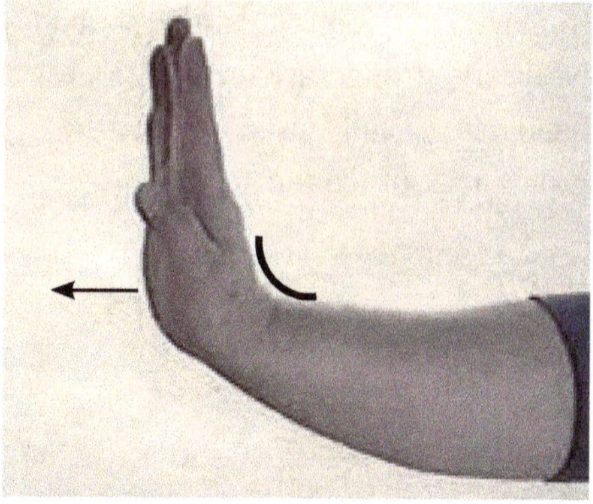

This hand shape can be used with the fingers pointed in any direction to allow the palm access to a large variety of targets. In this position, the area between the wrist and back of the hand may also be used in a hooking manner.

FUNDAMENTAL SHAPES

Knife hand [TAO SHOU 刀手]

AKA: Shuto [JAP] (knife hand) or Seiryu Toh [JAP] (palm edge).

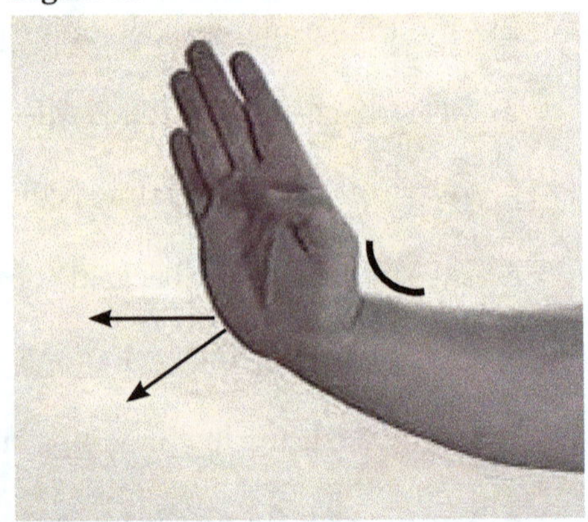

Figure 39

The knife hand (figure 39) is a shape that uses the edge of the palm (between the pinky and the wrist) to strike. This shape can be used in a thrusting, cutting, or chopping manner. The knife hand is used with the hand rotated in any position needed to strike the desired target. The knife hand position shown in figure 28 is for striking forward and/or downward to attack targets such as the collar bone. If the palm was facing upward or downward, it would be used to attack targets such as the neck or ribs.

Ridge hand [BEI TAO SHOU 背刀手]

AKA: Hirabasami [JAP] (inside ridge hand).

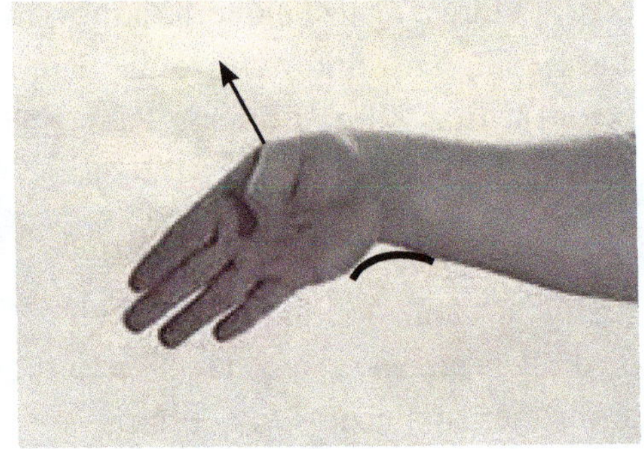

Figure 40

The ridge hand (figure 40) is a hand shape that uses the part of the hand opposite the edge, between the base of the thumb and the index finger's first joint to strike with. Not very strong structurally, ridge hands are usually used against the groin, neck or temple.

BACKHAND [SHOU PEI 手背]

AKA: Haishu [JAP] (back-hand).

The back of the hand (figure 41) is used to strike sensitive areas such as the face, groin, or ribs. This shape is used with opening arc techniques.

Figure 41

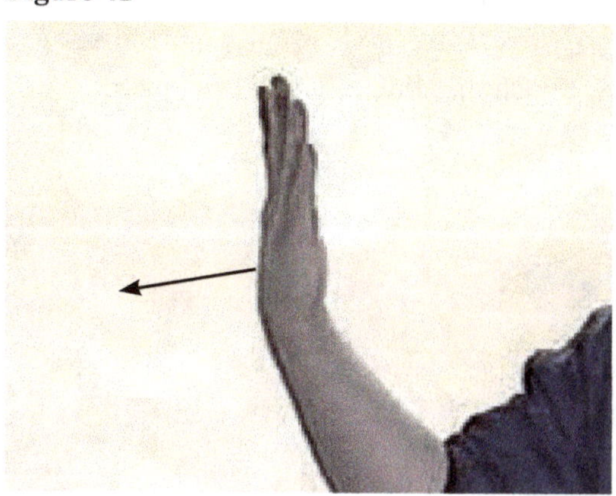

SPEAR HAND [CH'IANG SHOU 槍手]

AKA: Nukite [JAP].

The spear hand (figure 42) is a hand shape that utilizes the fingertips in a thrusting manner, targeting soft areas and nerve centers like the throat and armpit. There are times when the spear hand shape is used to rake an opponent's eyes. Spear hands can be in various shapes, ranging from a single finger to all four. Shown is a standard vertical spear hand.

Figure 42

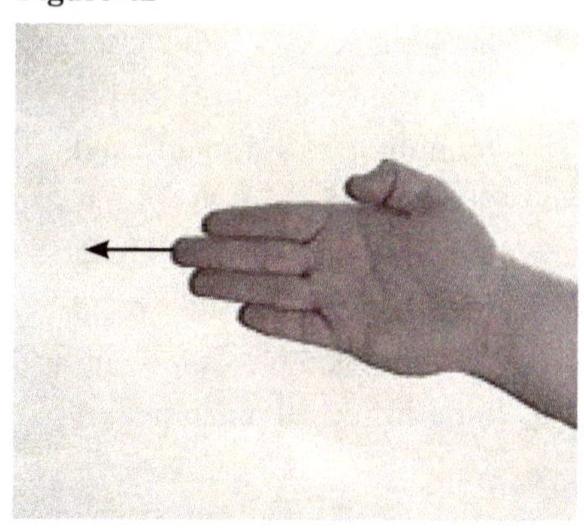

FUNDAMENTAL SHAPES

Tiger's Mouth [Hu k'ou 虎口]

AKA: Hirabasami [JAP] (inside ridge hand).

The tiger's mouth (figure 43) is used in a number of striking, and grabbing actions. As a strike, it is usually aimed at soft targets such as the neck. It is also used when manipulating an opponent's limbs. The tiger's mouth is usually a precursor to a palm strike or clawing/grabbing actions (Eagle, Tiger, or Dragon).

Figure 43

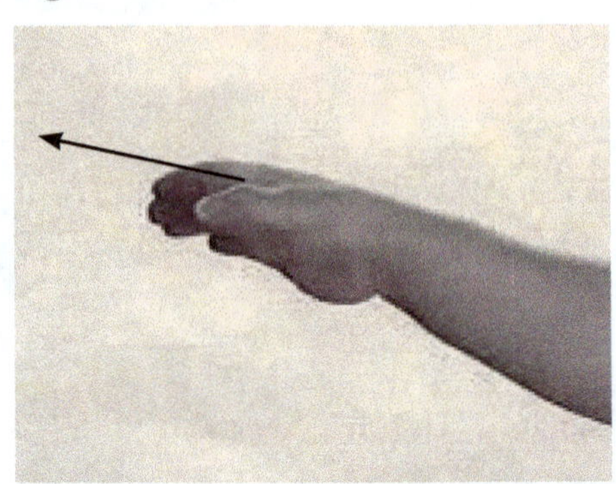

Rigid Palm

AKA: Single Finger Bridge Hand [T'an Chih Ch'iao Shou 單指橋手], Single Finger Contemplation and Pearl Bridge.

The rigid palm (figure 44) is essentially a fully closed tiger claw with the index finger extended. The rigid palm is used for striking, grabbing, and hooking actions. This is an important hand position for training one's fingers and "Bridge" (forearms). Prominently used in the Hung Family Systems, this hand position also has some cultural/historical meanings.

Figure 44

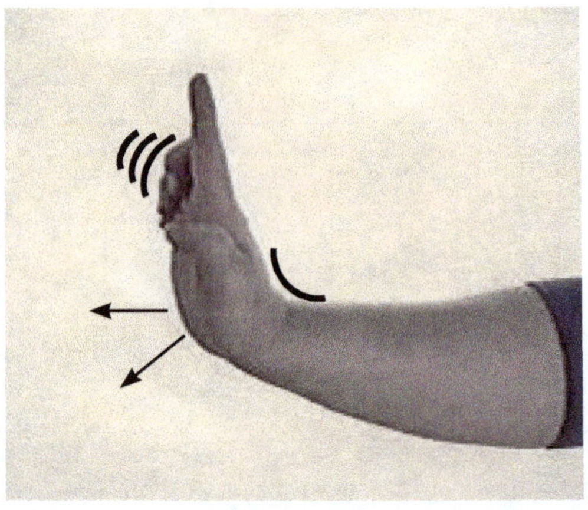

TIGER CLAW [HU CHIAO 虎爪]

The tiger claw (figure 45) is the most basic and popular claw shape in martial arts. The tiger claw can be used to attack in many diverse ways. Tiger claws are initially practiced as a sinking, clawing action, immediately following a palm strike. It is also employed in grabbing, tearing, and manipulating actions. In the tiger claw shown, the fingers are just past clawing and in the grabbing stage.

Figure 45

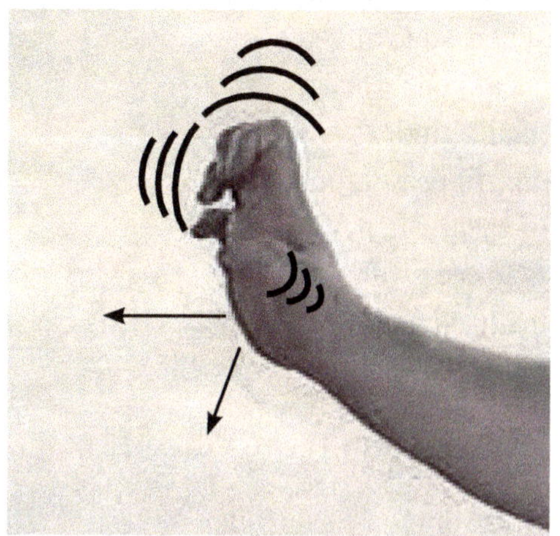

EAGLE CLAW [YING CHIAO 鷹爪]

Figure 46

The eagle claw (figure 46) is a specialized claw used to seize and tear cylindrical targets such as the trachea, biceps, or triceps. When grabbing a target such as a biceps, the finger tips are placed on the internal bicipital furrow to attack the nerves and blood vessels.

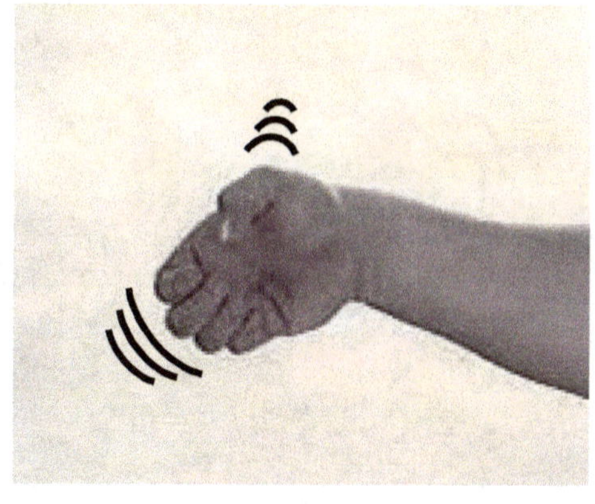

FUNDAMENTAL SHAPES

Eagle beak [Ying chou 鷹咮]

AKA: Yubi Basami [JAP] (knuckle/fingertip strike).

The eagle beak (figure 47) is a specialized eagle claw for attacking areas such as the trachea or subclavian triangle. When attacking the trachea, one inserts the thumb, index, and middle fingers around the trachea. Then, using this grab as a fulcrum, sink

Figure 47

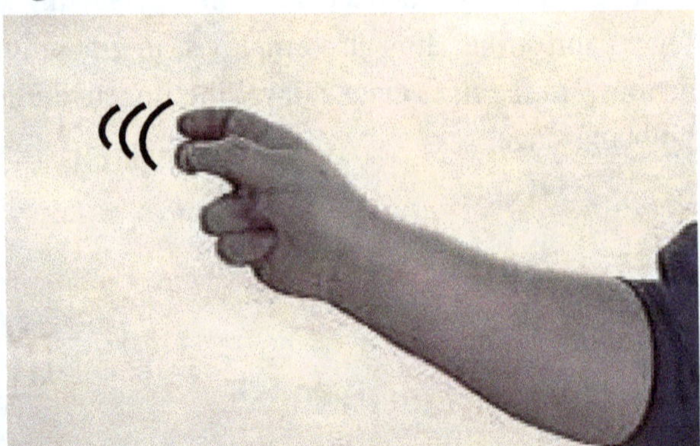

the hand and bend the wrist. This causes the second knuckles of the ring and pinky to press into the trachea.

Dragon claw [Lung chiao 龍爪]

The dragon claw (figure 48) is like a tiger claw in that it is often used in conjunction with a palm strike; however, the fingers are used in a similar fashion to an eagle claw. Following striking, and grabbing, dragon claws use a tearing action by sinking or accelerating the wrist away from the target.

Dragon claws are also used in blocking, striking, and hooking actions. This hand shape is very useful in grasping techniques when manipulating an opponent's limbs for Ch'in-Na or Shuai purposes.

Figure 48

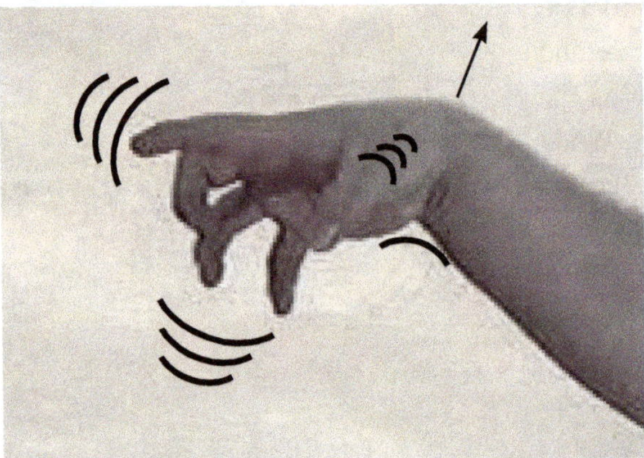

Many systems use Dragon claws in slightly different shapes. The Dragon claw shown is with a bent wrist to illustrate hooking and striking points.

CRANE HEAD [HE T'OU 鶴頭]

AKA: Crane beak [He tsui 鶴鶴]

Figure 49

The crane's head (figure 49) is a hand position mimicking the head of a White Crane. This is a hand position that uses single (index finger) or multiple fingertips (pressed together) in a pecking manner to attack soft targets and nerves. The back of the wrist is used for striking and the area of the wrist and palm for hooking.

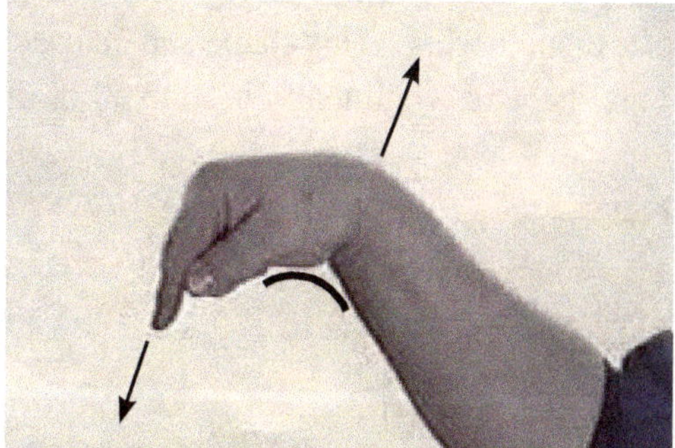

This shape is prominently used in Hung-Chia Ch'üan, Pai-He Ch'üan (all branches), and Go-Ju Ryu. Shown is a crane's head with the index finger and thumb pressed together.

PRAYING MANTIS HOOK [T'ANG LANG K'OU 螳螂鉤]

The praying mantis hook (figure 50) mimics the front limbs of the praying mantis. A praying mantis hook is used primarily for trapping limbs; it is also a recoiled position for striking. The shape is similar to a Crane's head with the palm more vertical and is used in similar ways.

Figure 50

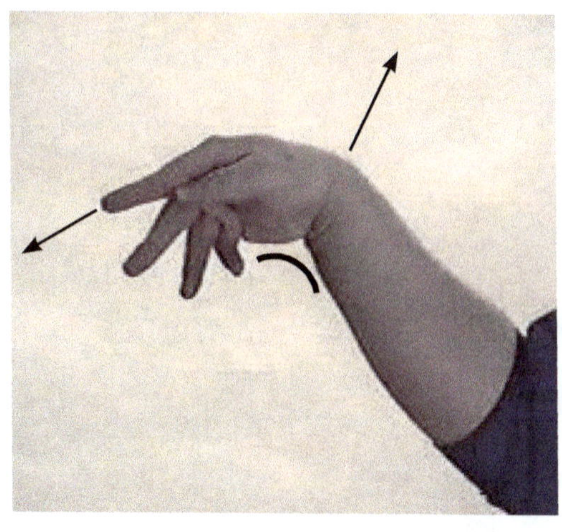

FUNDAMENTAL SHAPES

The crane's wing (figure 51) hand shape mimics the shape and movements of a crane's wing. This shape can be used for hooking, blocking, and striking. This shape is prominently used in all of the White Crane systems.

Figure 51

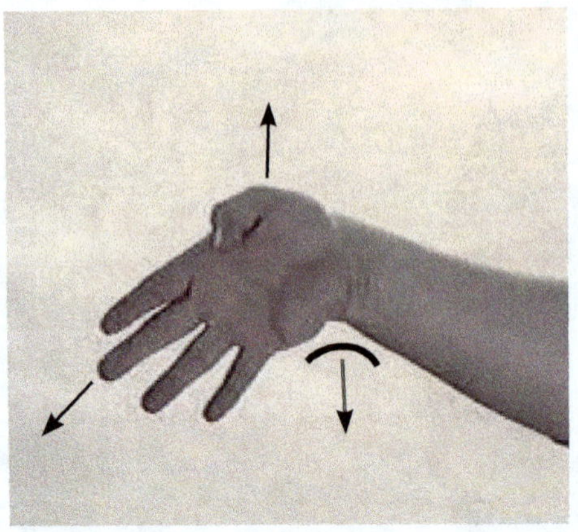

STANCES - CORE STRUCTURE, THEORY, AND TRAINING

STANCE [SHIH 勢] VS. STEP [PU 步]

Stance is one of the most important training tools a martial artist has; it is the foundation of all physical skills associated with these arts. There are two widely used Chinese terms for martial arts stances. Shih 勢, which means stance or posture, describes static stances, and Pu 步 (pronounced boo), which means step, describes dynamic stance work. In Pai-Chia Ch'üan, we prefer to use Pu; it promotes the idea that stance or stance work must be active and alive, full of energy, even when standing "still."

William Luciano (Pai-Chia Ch'üan) and Sharif Anael-Bey (Hung-Ga Kuen) demonstrating and co-teaching proper stance training at the Saratoga Martial Arts Festival in 2013.

STANCE TRAINING [BU-FA 步法]

The initial goals of stance training are strengthening the legs, improving balance, increasing endurance, developing a stable center of gravity, and making one's natural stepping/standing methods contain the essence of classical stance structures. These are essential building blocks for a strong martial foundation. Holding stances statically for specific periods of time is where we learn about core structure and stability. Shifting, turning, stepping, and jumping from one stance to another is where we learn about the dynamic qualities of stances. Proper stance training allows us to put our mass in motion, guiding and directing where we want to go.

Another skill acquired through stance training is the ability to be both stable and mobile at the same time. One should be able to "sink" their stance so as to be difficult to be moved by an opponent (rooting). At the same time one should be able to accelerate in any direction, to any other stance, so that we may evade or flank an opponent.

Stance training also allows us to efficiently create energy with our legs, amplify that energy, and with proper hip work, transfer that energy to the core of

77

our body where it can be amplified more and directed to our anatomical weapons for issuing to an opponent. Conversely, proper stance work will allow us to receive and dissipate energy, with the legs acting like shock absorbers.

CLASSIFICATION OF STANCES

Stances can be classified as back-weighted, neutral/even-weighted, forward-weighted, or transitional. In fact, when one takes a step forward, they are essentially going from a neutral position through a back-weighted, even-weighted, forward-weighted, and neutral position. When we walk, we repeat this process over and over.

STRUCTURE

The structure of any stance must be correct. By correct, we mean done in a way that is not harmful to the joints and will allow energy to pass through the legs and hips efficiently with minimal friction. I personally know of a number of martial artists that have ruined their knees from improper training.

THE FOOT [CHIAO 腳]

The ball, bottom of the heel, and the outside-bottom edge of the foot are what connect you to the ground; you want the weight of the body to transfer directly from the leg into the ground. That means the foot needs to be absolutely flat on the ground. You do not want the foot everted (when the sole of the foot is rotated outward and upward away from the midline) as this will lift the blade edge and press the arch downward. Nor do you want the foot inverted (when the sole of the foot is rotated inward and upward toward the midline) too much as this will lift the arch, increasing the potential for rolling and damaging the ankle.

THE LEG [T'UI 腿]

The leg has the job of connecting the foot to the hip, with the knee being the weak link in the middle. Because of the amount of energy passing through the legs, the knees must align correctly.

The photos in figure 52 show three leg positions with the knee bent forward. In leg position A., the knee is flexed inward, putting it inside the line between the hip and the foot. This is a very poor position that will eventually damage the knee. A strike from the outside of the leg in this position will severely damage the knee. A warning

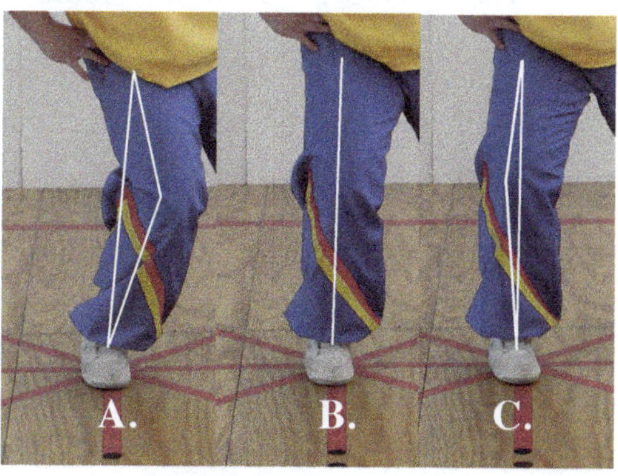

Figure 52

sign of the leg being in this position is the foot being in an everted position. Leg position B. is the most natural position with the hip, leg, and foot aligned. This position is very strong front to back. Leg position C. has the knee flexed slightly outward of the hip-foot line. This position allows a little more structure to absorb strikes against the outside of the leg. The outside bottom edge of the foot is pressed downward, creating a slight inversion of the foot. As long as the bottom edge of the foot is in contact with the ground, this is structurally ok. This leg position is also valuable for training skills used in leg trapping and takedowns.

THE HIP [K'UA 胯]

The K'ua comprises the pelvis and the groin. The top of the pelvis is where the spine attaches, and the bottom is where the legs attach. The K'ua is a very important and, in general, slightly misunderstood part of stance work. Proper hip work allows most of the energy created by the legs to be utilized by the upper part of the body (waist and torso); it also allows the energy produced on one side of the body to be received or issued on the other side.

When training, the tailbone should be tucked under, with the hips curled slightly forward using the lower abdominal muscles and obliques. You must feel your way through this process; the subtle qualities take time to articulate accurately.

The bottom of the K'ua and the top of the thighs, where the femur connects to the pelvis, are responsible for four significant actions:

1. The legs move forward (parallel to the Saggital plane).

FUNDAMENTAL SHAPES

2. The legs move backward (parallel to the Saggital plane).

3. Opening the K'ua [k'ai k'ua 開胯] consists of the front of the thighs rotating, twisting, or expanding laterally (away from the Median plane).

4. Closing the K'ua [he k'ua 合胯] consists of the front of the thighs rotating, twisting, or contracting medially (towards the Median plane).

STANCE TERMINOLOGY

Terminology associated with stance work is used for teaching and learning purposes. It allows consistent structural criteria to be met. A stance is designated as a right or left stance by the foot that is forward. Forward is defined as the direction of your opponent, perceived or real. A fight line is an imaginary line connecting your anatomical center to your opponent's anatomical center. As discussed earlier, stance [shih] and step [pu] are two words used to define stance in Chinese martial arts. Stance defines the static shapes of standing used in martial arts. Structurally, a stance is a combination of alignments from the feet to the top of the hips used for specific purposes in martial training. Step defines dynamic shapes of standing and stepping.

Other important terms associated with learning and teaching stance-work are:

Posture [shih 勢] - Posture is the entire body; essentially, how the spine, shoulders, arms, and head are aligned and combined with stance/step.

Base [ti p'an 底盤] - The area between the feet. Literally: domain, a territory under one's control, the foundation of a building, or base of operation.

Foot-length, foot width, and fist-width - When measuring the width and depth of our stances, the unit of measurement we use is one's own foot length. Foot width/fist-width are also used at times, and both are approximately equal to one-third of a foot length. Stances are measured from heel to heel.

Depth and width - Depth is the distance between the feet front to back on the fight centerline. Width is the distance between your feet side to side, perpendicular to the fight centerline.

Shallow and deep - These are terms used when talking about the depth of a stance. Shallow is when the distance between the feet is short front to back. Deep is when the distance between the feet is long, front to back.

Mild and severe - Are terms used to describe severity in the width, depth, and height of a stance. Mild is when a stance is not extreme; for example, a mild Bow Stance (AKA Gung-Pu or Bow and Arrow Stance) is not very deep, narrow, or low. Severe is when a stance is extreme; a Bow Stance that is deep, narrow, and very low would be considered severe. The more severe the stance, the harder it is to attain proper foot and hip position.

Coverage - This is a term used to describe mildness or severity in stance width. Coverage describes how a stance is viewed from the front at ground level. The photos in figure 53 show three different levels of coverage, with the Side Horse Stance on the top being covered, the Five Star Stance in the middle being partially covered, and the Bow Stance on the bottom being uncovered.

These terms may also be used when referring to accessibility to anatomic targets. For example, in a covered stance, the groin is not easily accessible. In an uncovered stance, the groin is easily accessible.

Full and Empty - Full is when all of the weight and/or energy is in one leg. Empty is when all of the weight and/or energy is out of one leg. Filling is when the weight and/or energy is shifting from one leg to the other; the leg receiving the weight or energy is called the filling leg. The filling leg is also called the issuing leg if the step becomes a kick.

Figure 53

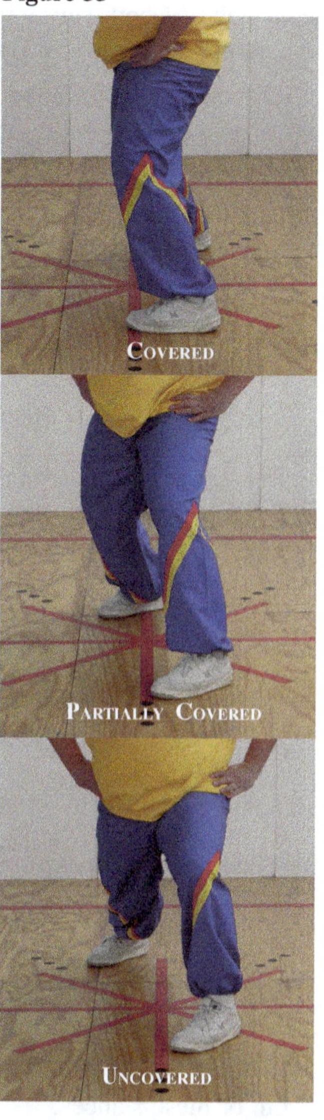

          FUNDAMENTAL SHAPES

Even Weighted Stances

Fifty-fifty, or even weighted stances, are very good training tools for the beginning martial artist. They are the easiest stance shapes to learn. Balance and stability, both very important aspects of stance training, are also easier to attain in even weighted stances. The torso, being in the center of one's base (T'i-Pan), allows for good "Rooting" practice as well. Even weighted stances are easier to move from. Either foot can step. Both knees need to be bent and, when practicing techniques from even weighted stances, it is easier to feel which leg is creating energy.

The eight primary even weighted stances are:

1. Attention Stance

2. Natural/Ready Stance

3. Ma Pu - Horse Stance

4. Pa Pu - Character Eight Stance

5. Fang Pu - Front (square) Stance

6. San Chien Pu - Three Battles Stance

7. Tun Pu - Squat Stance

8. Wu-Hsing Pu - Five Star Stance

The first two stances in this category, attention and natural stances, are very easy to articulate. Attention stance is when the feet are together, toes pointing straight ahead. Natural or ready stance is when you stand with your feet shoulder-width apart, parallel and pointing straight ahead. This is a natural standing position. Many techniques, salutations, self-defenses, and training forms are taught from these positions. The hips should be tucked forward in both of these stances. The legs should be straight, and the knees should not be locked out.

HORSE STANCE [MA PU, MA BU 馬步]

AKA Ssu P'ing Ma [四平馬 Four (angle) Flat Horse], Kiba Dachi [JAP]

Ma pu (figure 54), or horse stance (horse riding step), is the most important stance in Chinese martial arts. All stances have elements of horse stance in them. Side horse stance [邊馬步 pian ma pu, bian ma bu] and angled side horse stance are two variations.

In some southern-style schools, the terms horse and stance are synonymous. It is not uncommon to see a number of stances in a particular system have horse [ma] as part of the name, i.e., twisted horse, hanging horse, leaning horse, etc.

Horse stance is three-foot lengths wide, zero-foot lengths deep. Feet are parallel, knees well bent (forward) and pressed to the sides (not rotated to the sides as this will move the knee in a backward direction, expose the inside of the knee and make the toes point /feet turn outward). The hips should be tucked (curled) forward with the spine erect. Weight should be evenly distributed (50% on the right, 50% on the left) with pressure being felt on the outside, bottom edge, of the feet. The anal sphincter should be tight, and the feet should grip the ground.

Side horse stance is three-foot lengths deep, zero-foot lengths wide.

Figure 54

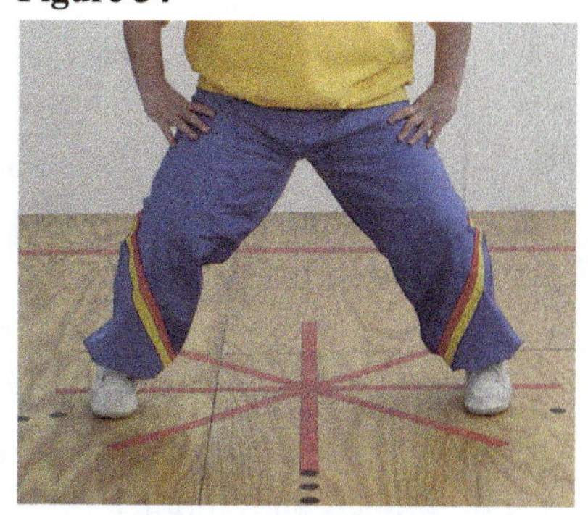

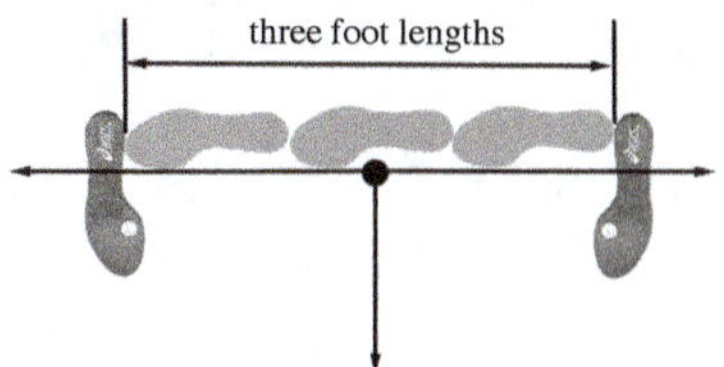

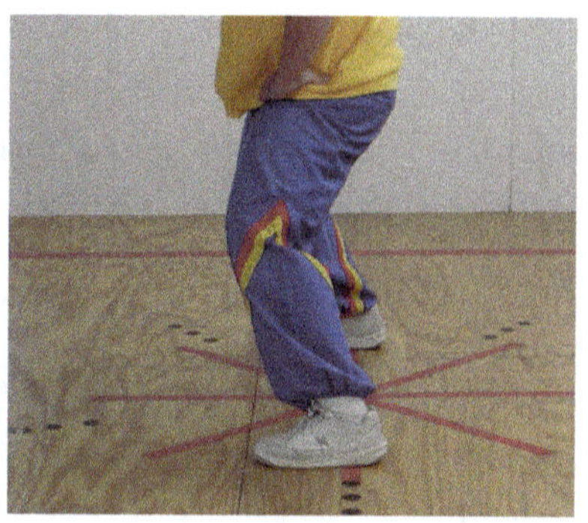

FUNDAMENTAL SHAPES

SQUAT STANCE [TUN PU 蹲步]

Figure 55

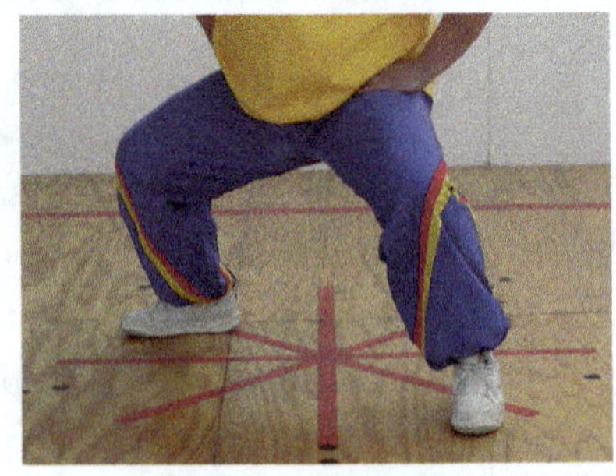

AKA Open Horse stance, Shiko Dachi [JAP] (squat stance), Seiunchin Dachi [JAP].

Tun pu or squat stance (figure 55) is similar to angled side horse stance except the feet are not parallel; they are perpendicular, the front foot points toward the opponent. The Squat Stance is very stable and rooted. It is used quite often to attack an opponent's legs while fighting in close quarters. This stance is similar to Pa-Chi Ch'üan's Half Horse Stance in appearance and application, although the weight distribution is slightly different.

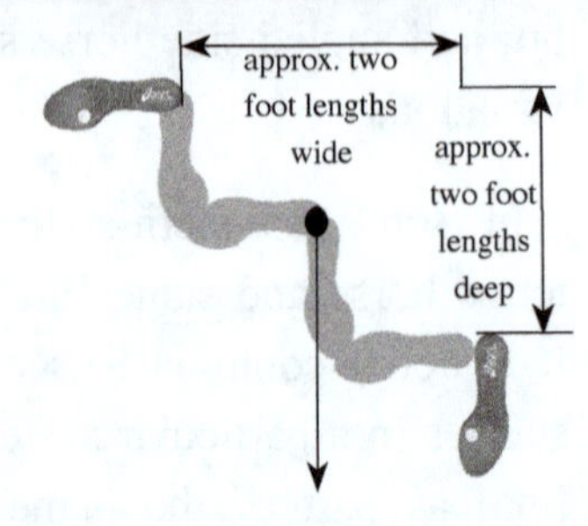

The Squat Stance is two-foot lengths deep and two-foot lengths wide. Knees are well bent (over the toes), with one bent in the forward direction and the other at ninety degrees. The hips should be tucked (curled) forward with the spine erect. Like Horse Stance, weight should be evenly distributed (50% on the right, 50% on the left) with pressure being felt on the outside, bottom edge of the feet. The anal sphincter should be tight, and the feet should grip the ground.

Figure 56

CHARACTER EIGHT STANCE [PA PU 八步]

AKA Goat Capturing stance, Hourglass stance, Uchi Hachiji Dachi [Japanese - inverted open leg stance].

Pa pu or character eight stance (figure 56), is very important for learning how to close the kua (hips), a key component of compacting and practicing turning skills. The name pa is used because the feet are in the same position as the character for eight. The basic version of this stance is two-foot lengths wide at the heels, with both feet and legs rotated inward from the hips.   When the knees are bent

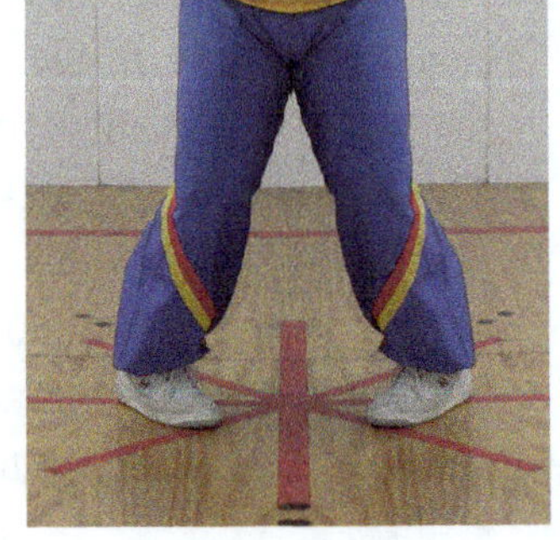

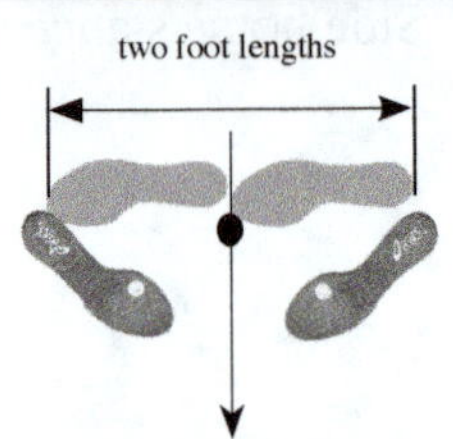

more and the thighs are closer together, this is also known as hourglass stance.

FRONT STANCE [FANG PU 方步]

AKA Square stance

Fang pu or front stance (figure 57) is an exceptional training stance. It allows for full extension of the limbs and rotation of the waist while at the same time allowing you to feel when the weight is transferring forward, backward, or to the sides.

Fang actually means square; we use that term because the basic version of this stance is two-foot lengths deep and two-foot lengths wide. Knees are well bent (forward) and flexed slightly to the outside of the hip-foot line. The hips should be tucked (curled) forward with the spine erect. Like horse stance, weight should be evenly distributed (50% on the right, 50% on the left) with pressure being felt on the outside, bottom edge of the feet. The anal sphincter should be tight, and the feet should grip the ground.

There are many variations of this stance that are utilized by southern Fukien, Kwantung, and Okinawan systems. Southern Dragon style utilizes a narrower version. Fukien white crane and many karate systems use a shorter version of this known as San chien pu (Three Battles Stance).

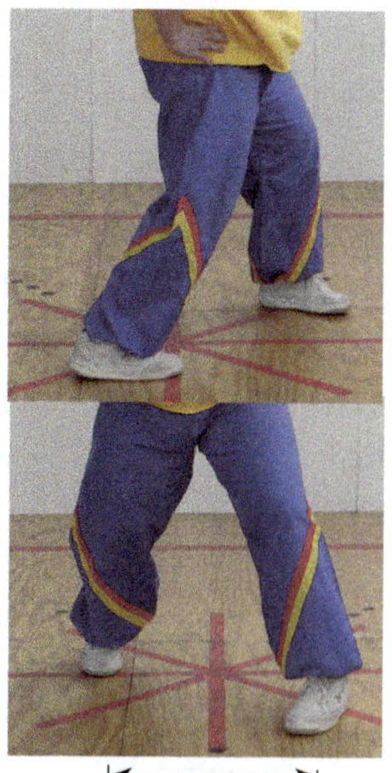

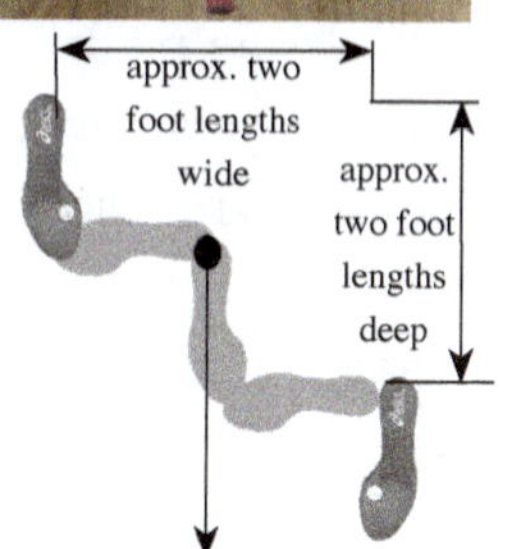

FUNDAMENTAL SHAPES

THREE BATTLES STANCE [SAN CHIEN PU 三戰步]

AKA Sanchin Dachi, Dragon stance

San chien pu or three battles stance (figure 58) is the primary training stance of Fukien White Crane, Five Ancestor's Fist, Uechi-Ryu, Go-ju-Ryu, and many other systems influenced by the Fukien fighting arts.

San chien pu has many variations; some methods prefer the back foot straight with the front foot at an angle while others prefer both feet toed in. Regardless of these differences, all styles practice rooting with this stance by "gripping" the ground with the feet.

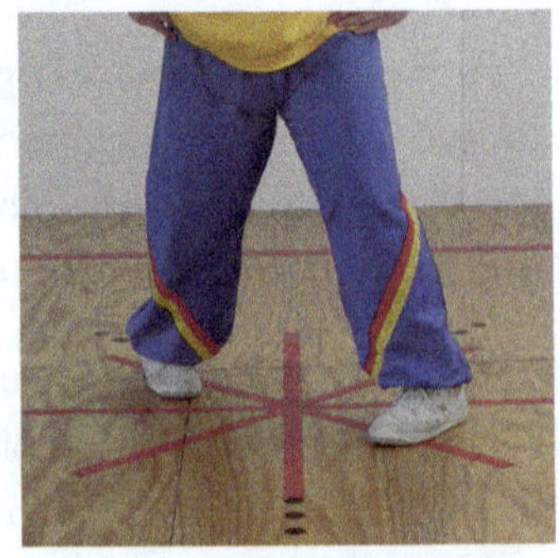

Figure 58

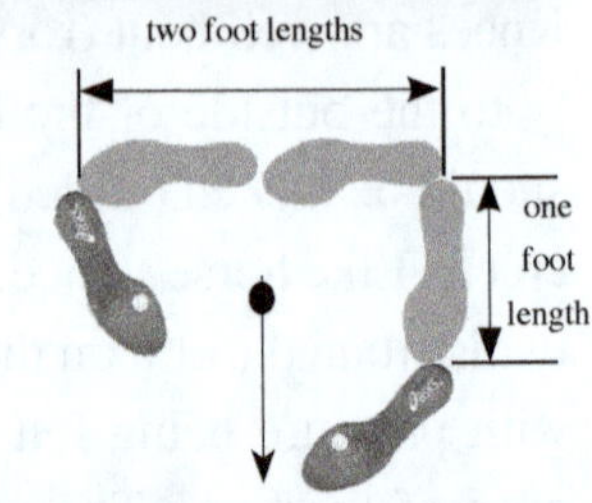

FIVE-STAR STANCE [WU HSING PU 五星步]

AKA Modified Fighting stance

Wu hsing pu or five-star stance (figure 59) is also known as "modified fighting stance" when the arms are held up in a guard position. It is very similar to the Neutral Bow stance from Ed Parker's Kenpo system. It is a combination of a side horse stance and a front stance. It has the offensive qualities of front stance and the defensive qualities of side horse stance. The feet are pointing approximately 45°; the torso is rotated toward the front so that the hips are at approximately 30° and the shoulders at 15°.

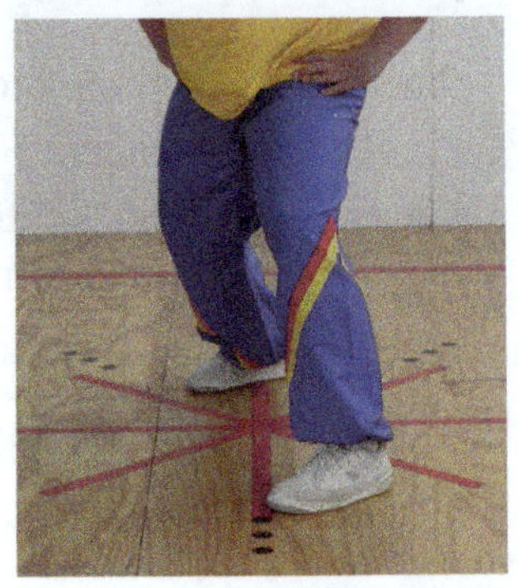

Figure 59

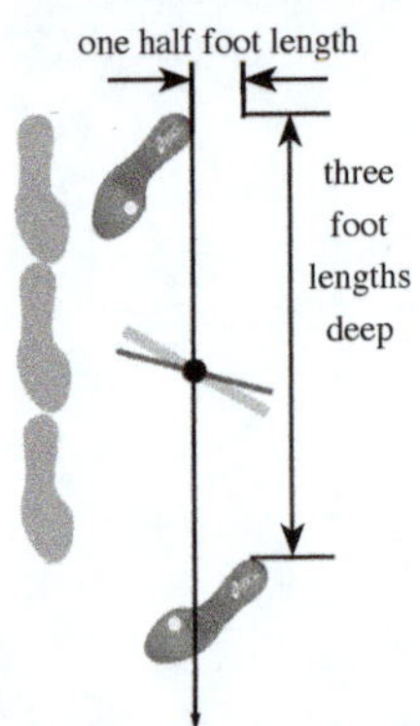

FORWARD WEIGHTED STANCES

As the name suggests. a forward weighted stance is any stance that has more weight on the forward leg, the one closest to our opponent. Forward weighted stances are usually an indication that you have shifted your weight forward after striking or to facilitate a kick with your rear leg. There are times when a forward weighted stance is a product of stepping backward or away from our opponent as a prelude to shifting back into an even or back weighted stance. This is often done as part of an 'open-close shuffle backward' or away from our opponent. In our art, there are three primary stances where the weight is obviously forward; bow stance, deep front or forward stance, and charging horse stance.

BOW STANCE [KUNG PU 弓步]

CHEST OPENING STANCE

[K'AI T'ANG PU 開膛步]

AKA Bow and Arrow stance [Kung Chien Pu 弓箭步] and Mountain climbing stance [Teng Shan Pu 登山步] (figure 60).

Bow stance is one of the primary training stances in Chinese martial arts. When moving forward, this stance trains the moving of your mass toward your opponent (requiring a step forward with the lead foot). This is often an explosive lunging action from a back-weighted or neutral weighted stance. This stance trains listening skills in the rear foot/leg when stepping backward, feeling the ground for proper placement.

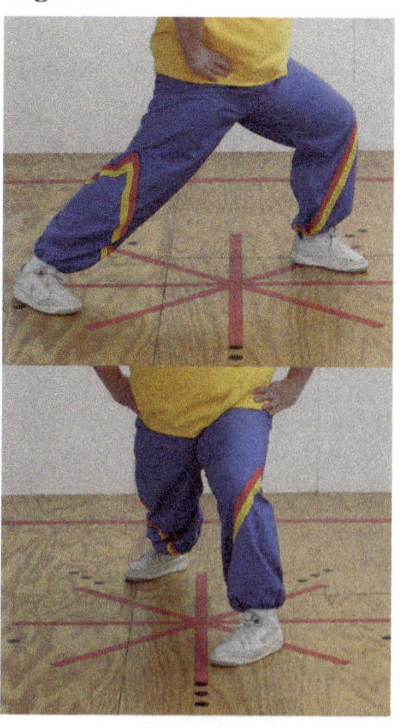

Figure 60

FUNDAMENTAL SHAPES

There are two primary variations of this stance. The first version, kung-pu, has the rear leg hip as far forward as the lead leg hip, and the torso is rotated toward the front foot. This is used when striking with the rear side hand or arm, pushing or striking with both hands and when preparing to kick with the rear leg. The second version, k'ai t'ang pu, has the lead leg, hip, and shoulder further forward than the rear leg hip. It is used when striking with the lead side arm.

For our basic training, a bow stance is four-foot lengths deep and one-foot length wide. The front leg knee is bent (forward), the rear leg is straight (but not locked out. The lead leg hip should be tucked (curled) forward, and the rear leg hip should be trying to tuck forward. Weight should be distributed (70% on the front, 30% on the rear) with pressure being felt on the outside, bottom edge of the feet. The anal sphincter should be tight, and the feet should grip the ground.

Figure 61

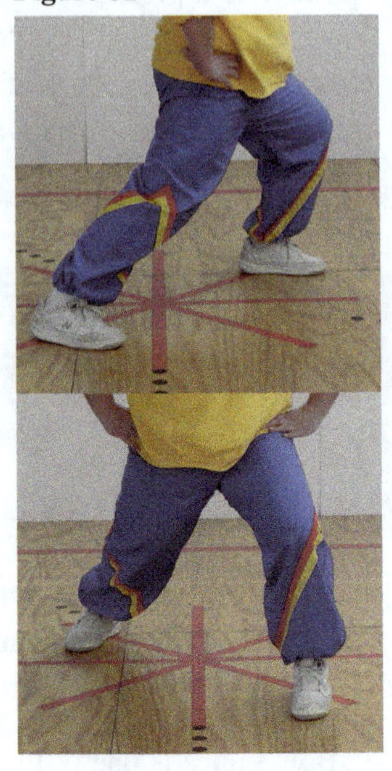

FORWARD STANCE [CH'IEN PU 前步]
AKA Deep Front stance, Forward Leaning stance, and Zenkutsu Dachi

A Forward stance (figure 61) is essentially a wide bow stance with the front foot pointing forward. This stance is used by many Oki-nawan, Japanese, and Korean striking arts. It is wide enough to allow the rear leg hip to easily rotate forward as the weight is shifted into the front leg. Often used when shifting forward from a squat stance and extending from a front stance.

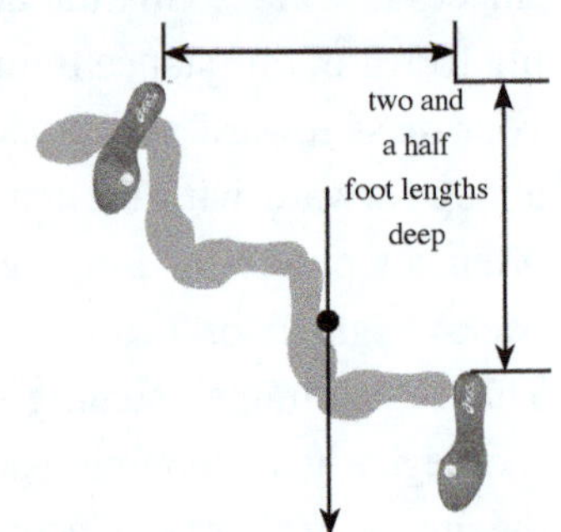

CHARGING HORSE STANCE

[CH'UNG MA PU 衝馬步]

Charging horse stance (figure 62) is the result of an explosive strike with the rear hand or arm where the rear leg hip, thigh, and torso are driven toward the target. It is essentially a front stance where the rear leg thigh is driven forward as the rear hip and shoulder are pulled toward the front hip. It is closely related to both front stance and twisted stance.

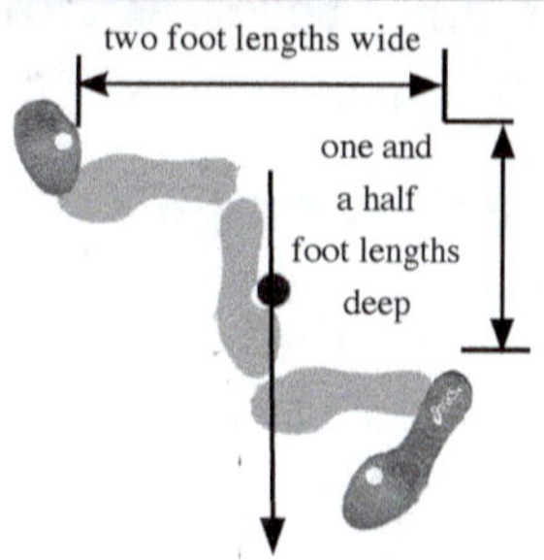

Back-Weighted Stances

As the name suggests. a back-weighted stance is any stance with more weight on the rear leg, the one furthest from our opponent. Back-weighted stances are a product of either extending a leg forward (to possibly kick with the stepping leg or initiate a strike with the lead arm) or shifting your weight to the rear foot (to evade, strike with the lead arm or kick with the lead leg). This stance is often used as part of an 'open-close' or 'close-open' shuffle forward or toward our opponent. In our art, there are many stances where most of the weight is obviously on the rear leg; cat stance, false step, crane stance, seven-star stance, four-six stance, crouching tiger stance, rear bow stance, twisted stance, and several other obscure stances.

Figure 63

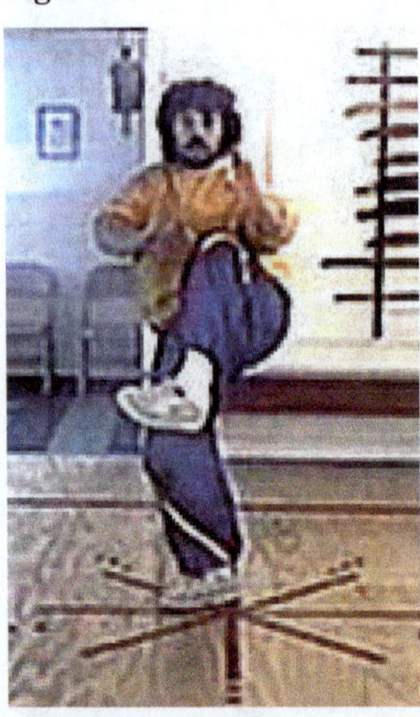

Figure 64

Crane stance [He Pu 鶴步]

AKA Golden Rooster Stands on One Leg, Hanging horse stance.

Crane stance (figures 63, 64) has 100% of the bodyweight on the back leg. Tactically, this is usually a product of the raised leg blocking, re-directing an attack, or chambering a kick. This stance is used to train balance and leg strength. Historically, it is said to have been used by Shaolin arts to counter the upward fighting techniques used by the Shaolin Leopard methods.

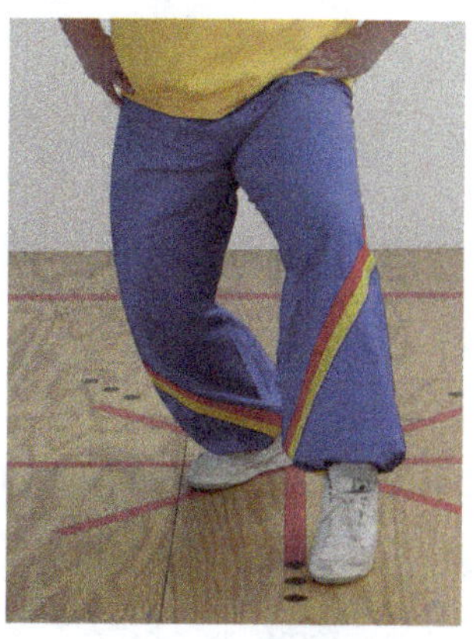

Cat stance [Mao Pu 貓步]

AKA Listening step [t'ing pu 聽步], False step [hsu pu 虛步].

Cat stance (figure 65) is the most popular of a series of back-weighted stances that have 0% to 40% of the body's weight on the front foot. The ball of the front foot is touching the ground with the heel up. The shape of the front foot looks like the back leg of a cat, which is where the name probably comes from. In general, this stance has no more than 10% of the body's weight on the front foot. Tactically, this stance allows for quick front leg kicks, blocking with the front leg, and jumping. There are also times when the front foot is "spot" loaded with 100% of the body's weight. An example of this would be when you drive the ball of the front foot into the ground as you lift the back foot and extend the rear leg backward in a retreating action.

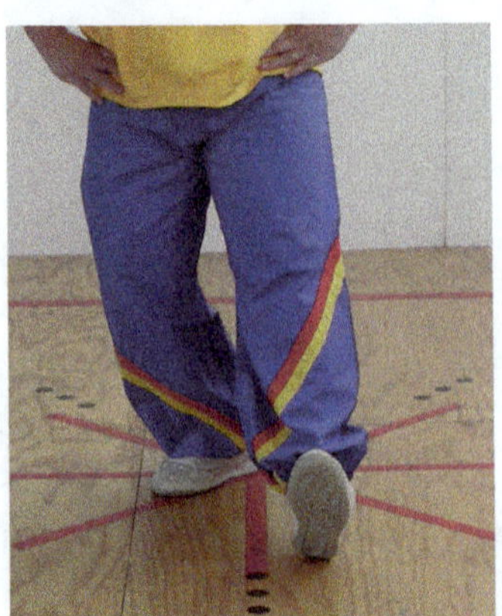

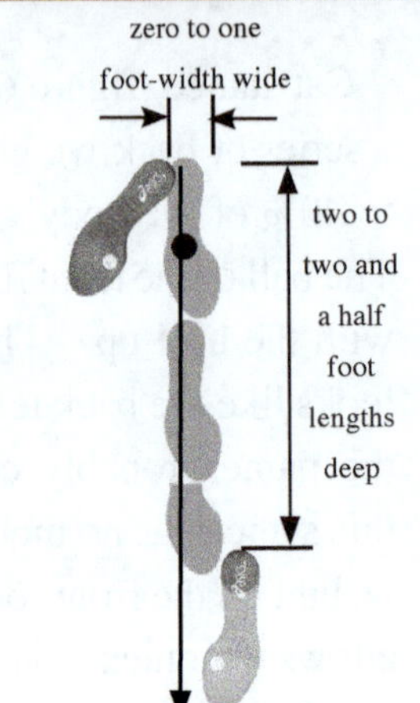

Seven-star stance [ch'i hsing pu 七星步]

Seven-star stance (figure 66), while used by many systems, is one of the primary stances of the Northern Praying Mantis systems.

The forward foot is approximately two to two and a half foot-lengths forward. The back leg is open approximately 45 degrees.

Like a cat stance, this stance generally has no more than 10% of the body's weight on the front foot. Tactically, this stance allows for quick front leg kicks, blocking with the front leg, and jumping.

The front foot position in a Seven-star stance is used to stomp with the heel; stop kick with the bottom of the foot, or hook an opponent's leg.

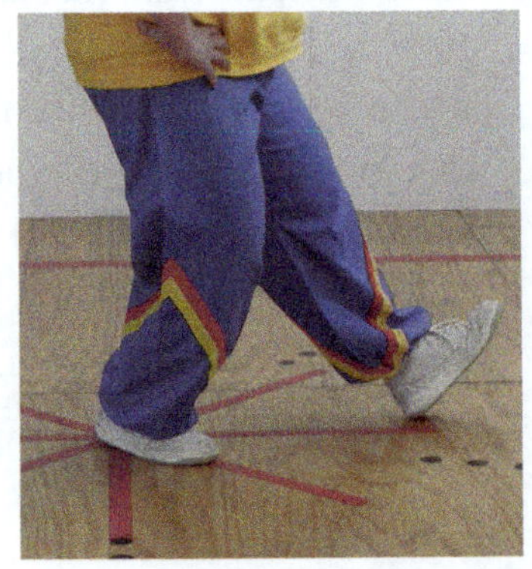

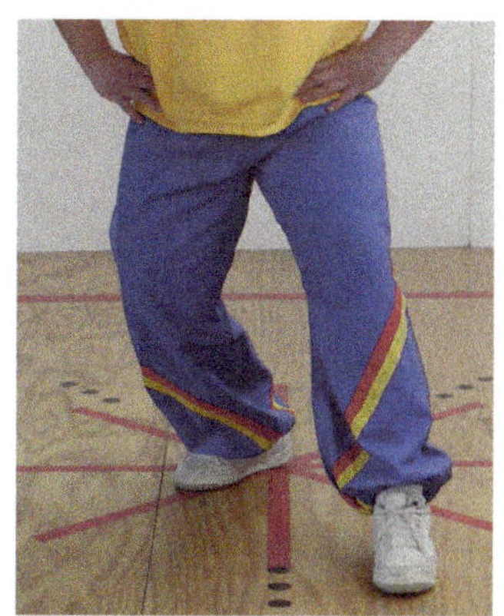

FALSE STEP [HSU PU 虛步]

A False step (figure 67) is one of a se-ries of back-weighted stances that that have 0% to 20% of the body's weight on the front foot. The front foot is flat on the ground.   A little more extended than a cat or seven-star stance, the front foot has 0% to 20% of the body's weight on the front foot.   Tactically, this stance al-lows for quick front leg kicks, blocking with the front leg, and jumping. There are also times when the front foot is "spot" loaded with 100% of the body's weight. An example of this would be when you drive the front foot into the ground as you lift the back foot and extend the rear leg backward in a retreating action.

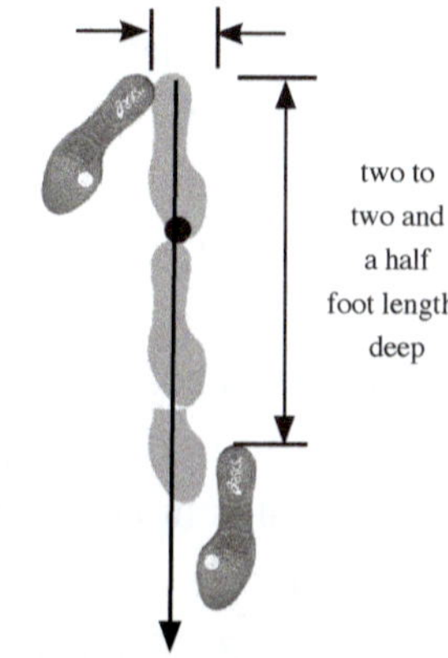

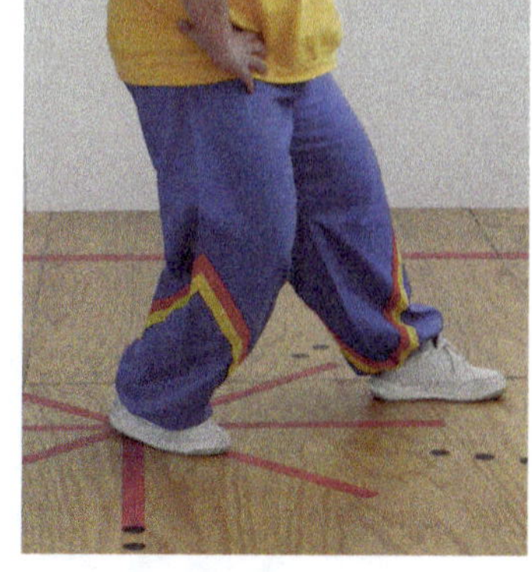

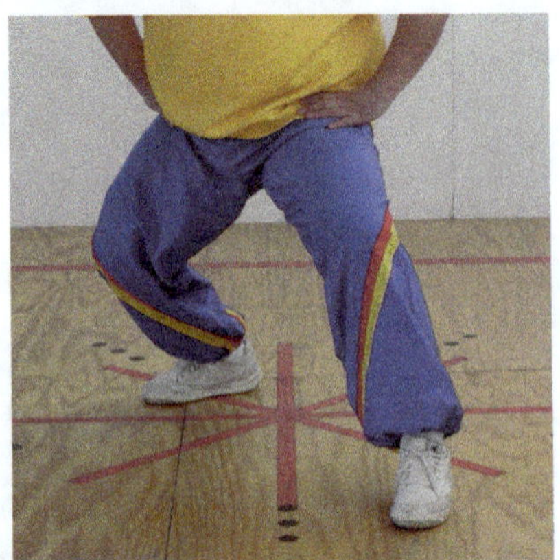

FOUR-SIX STEP [SSU-LIU PU 四六步]

Four-six stance (figure 68) is one of the classic back weighted stances in traditional Wu-Shu. It is essentially an angled side horse stance with the lead leg open, or an extended hsu pu with the rear leg kua opened a bit more. Weight distribution in a static version of this stance is approximately 40% of the weight on the front foot and 60% of the weight on the rear foot, hence the name, 4-6 stance. There is also a 3-7 stance [san-ch'i bu 三七步], which is in between a hsu pu and a ssu-liu pu.

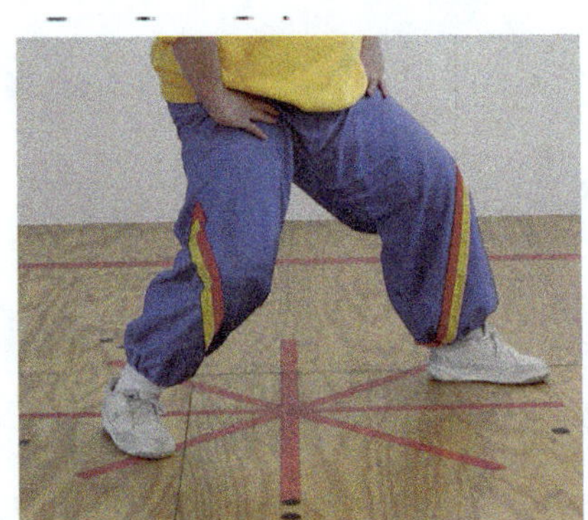

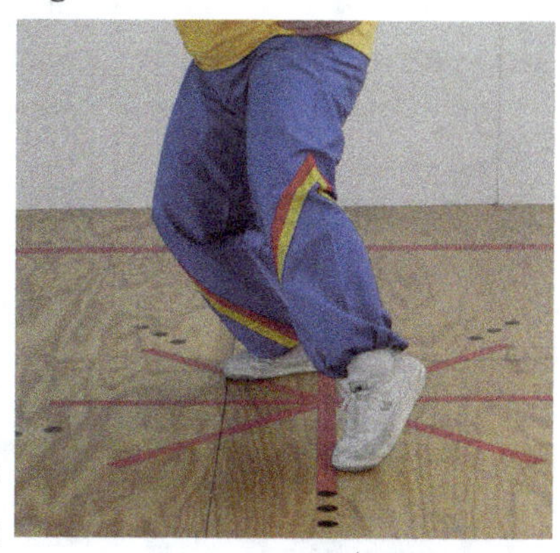

SIDE CAT STANCE [PIAN-MAO PU 邊貓步]

Side cat stance (figure 69) is as the name implies, an extended cat stance extending from the back foot through the outside-front quadrant of the front leg. It shares all of the qualities of a standard cat stance combined with the rotational qualities of a twisted stance.

There should be 0% to 40% of the body's weight on the front foot. The medial side of the ball of the front foot is touching the ground with the heel up.

In general, this stance has no more than 10% of the body's weight on the front foot. Tactically, this stance allows for quick front leg kicks, blocking with the front leg, and jumping.

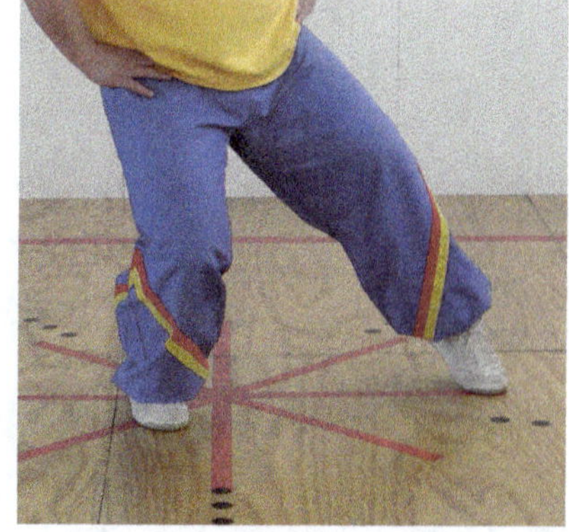

FUNDAMENTAL SHAPES

Taming Tiger stance (figure 70) is one of the classic back weighted stances in Chinese Martial arts. It is an extreme back weighted stance, with the front leg extended past the three foot-length distance. It could be also be considered a Gung-Pu with all of the weight shifted to the rear leg.

Figure 70

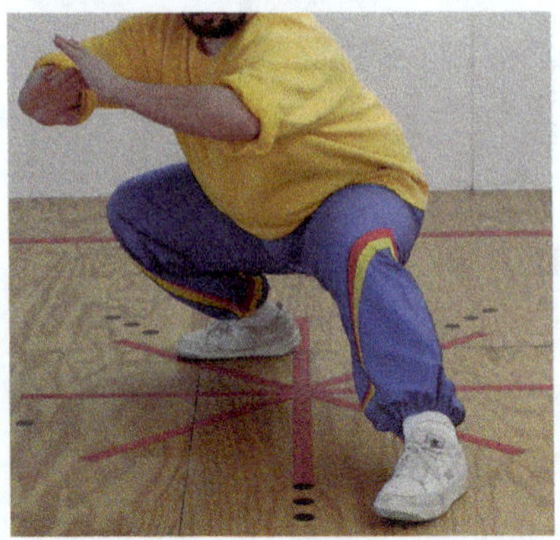

Figure 71 shows how the Taming the Tiger stance is used in conjunction with a Bow stance.

Figure 71

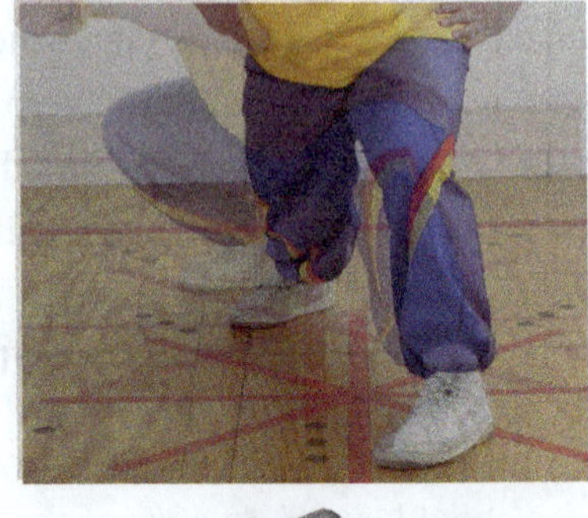

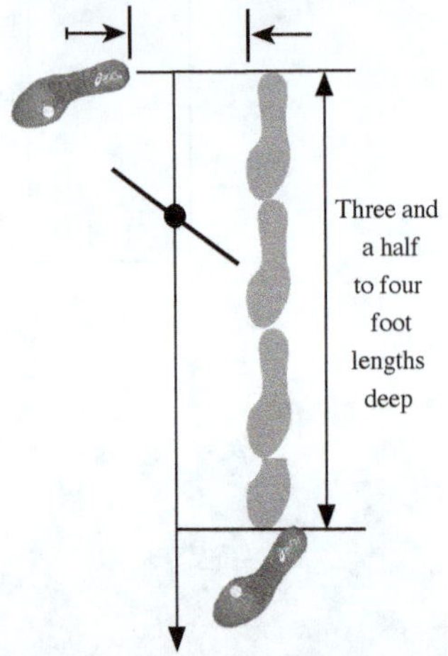

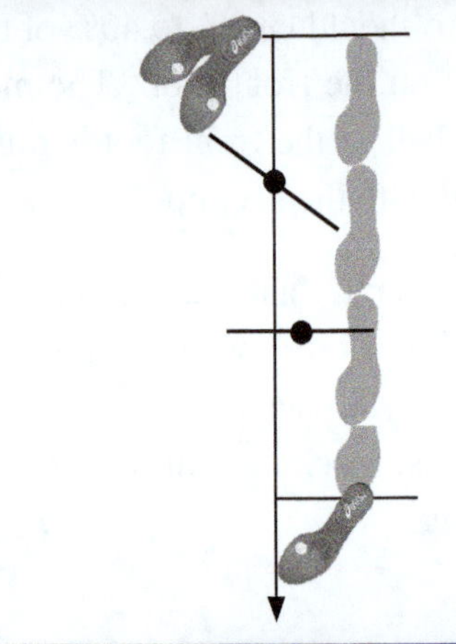

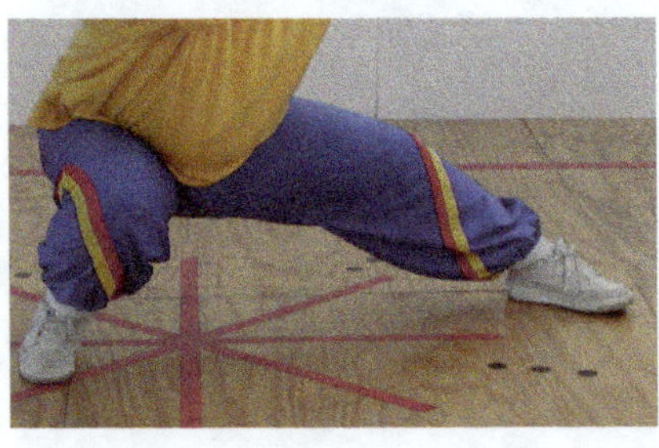

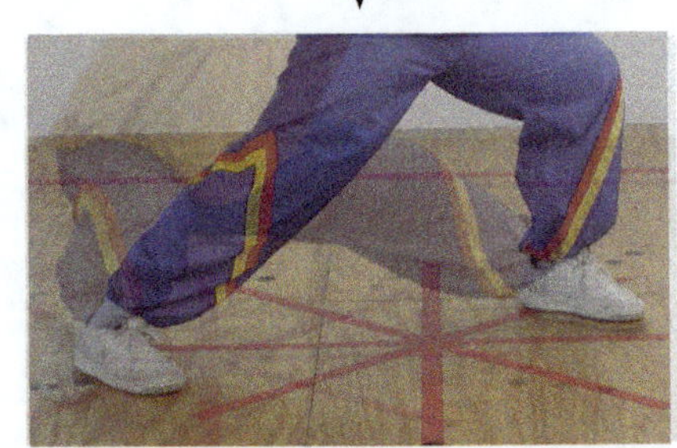

TWISTED STANCE [PAN PU 盤步]

Figure 72

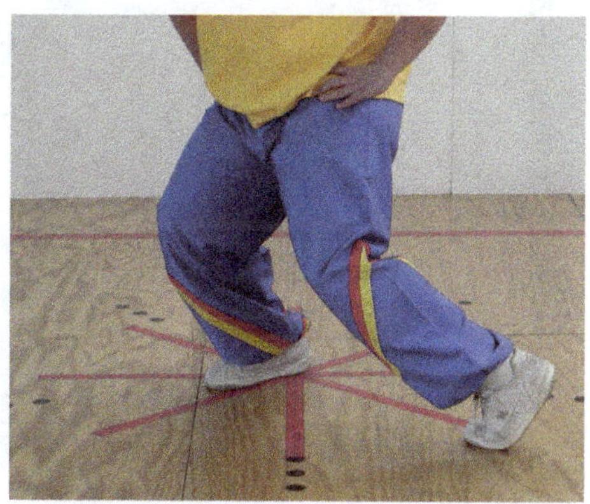

AKA Small (1/2) Twisted stance [Hsiao pan pu 小盤步]

Twisted stance (figure 72) plays a prominent role in the Pai-based arts. The quick body rotation and weight shift from side to side are primary tools in training the practitioner's ability to create and issue force. It should not be trained in a static posture; instead, it should focus on the dynamic shifting of the weight from leg to leg. It is very similar contextually to the "rotate the torso by pulling" [Ch'e-Shen[WG] 扯身] skill from the Tibetan White Crane system [Pak Hok Pai [CAN] 白鶴派].

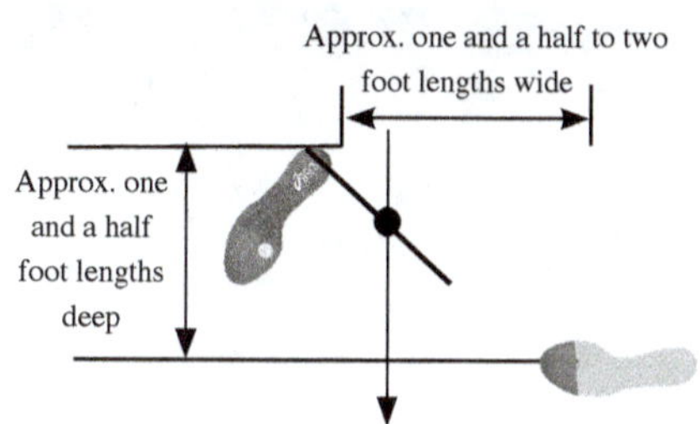

LARGE TWISTED STANCE [TA PAN PU 盤步]

A Large (full) twisted stance (figure 73) is primarily a transitional step, or stance. It has many variations that are based on how the posture is attained. Three of the more popular being: Crossed leg or Female stance [nu pu 女步] (stepping in front of, or behind the opposite leg into a crossed-leg posture), Coiling dragon stance [pan lung pu 盤龍步] (a full twisting action around one's virtical axis, into the posture, often pressing the legs together), and Dragon shaped step [lung hsing pu 龍形步] (opening the Kua and following the foot as if stepping around a post).

Figure 73

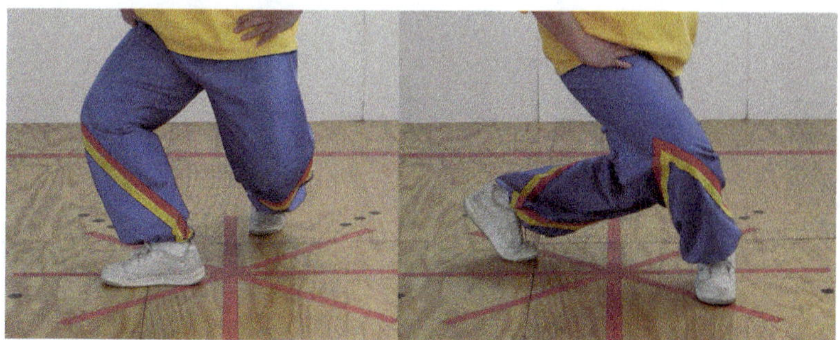

FUNDAMENTAL SHAPES

David L. Smith demonstrating the last techniques and posture from the form Pai-Lum (Pai-Lung Ch'üan) 1979.

- Photo by Martin Pickands

VI FUNDAMENTAL TRAINING:
Form Sequences

Forms, Form Sequences

Daniel K. Pai probably did not learn many form sequences during his early training. He grew up in a rough area; learning martial arts was not an activity; it was life preservation! The bulk of the training was application-based, learning and training how to fight. Drills, exercises, and form sequences were ways to train the body in movements and skills associated with fighting. Public demonstrations and cultural events such as Chinese New Year celebrations were the only times this type of training was performed publicly.

Daniel K. Pai teaching "Dragon Playing with Seven Stars," Windgap, PA, 1985

- Photo by Gary LaVallee

Today, martial arts are practiced by many as an activity or exercise, a by-product of the arts adapting to today's culture. Due to a lack of understanding and purpose, form sequences are now practiced primarily for demonstrations, competitions, and rank requirement reasons by many systems; martial form sequence training is quickly becoming extinct. It is disrespectful to the people and the systems these form sequences come from to allow these textbooks of martial skills to be practiced poorly and without purpose.

Training sequences [Lien Ch'üan Tao 練拳套]

As discussed at the beginning of chapter five, the Chinese word for form, shape, or appearance is Hsing [形]. The words Form, Shape, and Hsing describe the structure of something and how it looks. For example, if a martial artist or athlete moves correctly, they have good form. Shapes linked together dynamically with proper articulation, specific intent, and purpose are techniques. Techniques linked together are combinations; this is how we apply the art. Techniques arranged in solo training or paired practice patterns are referred to as a training sequence.

The proper term for a martial arts training sequence in Mandarin Chinese is Lien Ch'üan-Tao [練 拳 套]; it is often abbreviated to just Ch'üan. Lien [練] means to practice or drill. Ch'üan [拳] means fist; however, it also describes training sequences (Liu-Chia Ch'üan, Lien-Pu Ch'üan, etc.) and boxing systems (Lung-Hsing Ch'üan, T'ai-Chi Ch'üan, etc.). Tao [套] means to wrap or group. Together, these terms imply boxing practice that is packaged.

Another term that is popular with contemporary Wu-Shu practitioners is Tao-Lu [套路]. Lu means road or line. When combined with Tao, it can mean routine. Many traditional arts use Lu to identify specific forms in a sequence, group, or system of form sequences. For example, Mei-Hua Tao Er-Lu [梅花刀二路] means Plum Flower saber second road/routine. Two-person training sequences are called T'ui-Ta [隊打], which means team strike. Form, Set, Sequence, Routine, Kata (Japanese), and Hyung (Korean) are additional terms used when referring to Lien Ch'üan Tao, although the most common practice is to refer to these sequences as Forms.

Form sequences are textbooks containing techniques and theories characteristic of the style or system they represent. Almost every movement in a form is a potential strike, block, or grappling (joint locking, throwing, wrestling) maneuver. Form sequences should be practiced as organized shadow boxing, allowing practitioners to work on refining techniques alone. Some physical benefits of form training are leg strengthening, coordination, balance, proper breathing, and combining skills. Thomas St. Charles, a senior student of Daniel K. Pai, defined proper form training as a "Realistic practice of defense and counter-attack."

Forms have historical value in that they may contain hidden or "secret" techniques of the people who developed them. In some cases, they may offer insight into past training and fighting methods. For example, the form Kung-Tzu Fu-Hu Ch'üan [工字伏虎拳 I-Pattern Taming Tiger Fist], from the Hung-Chia system, is one of the oldest known form sequences in use today. It is said to have developed from one of the original Shaolin tiger forms.

FORM AND TRAINING SEQUENCE CATEGORIES

There are five types of training sequences, all of which can be trained either empty-handed or with weapons. These categories are Training, Fighting, Dummy, Health, and Two person forms. Some form sequences are combinations of these categories.

TRAINING FORMS:

Training forms use both sides of the body somewhat equally. They also tend to use two-handed techniques. Techniques in a training form are usually exaggerated and precise, though not always in an order that makes logical fighting sense. Training forms are primarily used as exercises to build coordination, strength, structure, and body dynamics.

FIGHTING FORMS:

Techniques in fighting forms are arranged in a logical,

strategic order to simulate attack and defense methods. There is usually a specific theory or principle that these routines adhere to. There is a tendency in this type of set to train one side of the body more than the other.

DUMMY FORMS:

In martial arts, a dummy is a mechanical training partner. Any training sequences practiced on an inanimate object is a dummy form. Some training dummies replicate parts of the human anatomy and may have arms and sometimes legs. Traditionally, these types of dummies are made from wood or metal. Dummies vary in appearance depending upon their use. Some additional types of dummies are wooden or iron posts, heavy bags, and speed bags. An advantage of training with these dummies is that techniques may be applied with full power without fear of injuring a live training partner. The main purpose of Dummy training is to provide feedback.

HEALTH FORMS:

Health forms promote physical development, breath control, and Ch'i development. These forms are considered a type of Ch'i-Kung and can be either Wai-Chia (external family) or Nei-Chia (internal family).

TWO-PERSON FORMS:

Two-person forms add a different dimension to form practice. Two-person forms can be as simple as back-and-forth drilling of techniques or as intricate as attack and counter-attack sequences. All training and fighting forms can and should be broken down into smaller two-person segments. Skills trained by two-person sets are:

a. Timing

b. Distance

c. Reaction

d. Creating and crossing Bridges

e. Logical counter techniques

f. Angles of attack and defense

g. Adapting to the various body types of training partners

Kung 公, Ta 大 , and Hsiao 小

In addition to form categories, there are different levels and variations of most form sequences. Modifiers are sometimes added to form names defining these variations. When Kung [公], which means public, is added to the sequence name, it implies a simplified or publicly taught version of that training form. Pai-Lin Ch'üan Kung would indicate a public or demonstration version of the form Pai-Lin Ch'üan. Forms may also be defined as major or minor sets. The Chinese terms for major and minor are Ta [大] and Hsiao [小]. Ta can mean larger, greater than, or more important. Hsiao means smaller, lesser than, or less important. We generally use these terms to differentiate between basic and advanced versions of the same form sequence. Pai-Lin Ch'üan Ta would imply an advanced or more refined version of the form Pai-Lin Ch'üan. Pai-Lin Ch'üan Hsiao would imply a fundamental or less refined version of the form Pai-Lin Ch'üan. These terms are pronounced Dai and Sho in Japanese, as in Bassai Dai and Bassai Sho.

103

TRAINING FORMS USED IN THE PAI FAMILY ARTS

There has been a lot of diversity in the training forms implemented or used in the Pai Family Arts over the years. Any technique, drill, or form sequence practiced using a Pai-based foundation (mechanics, structure, theory, etc.) is a Pai form regardless of origin. However, it would be ignorant not to know the source of a training routine. Knowing where things come from allows you to research a particular training set and see some of the skills from a different point of view. Form sequences practiced in the various Pai-based schools consist of original, borrowed, and new forms.

Original forms are training sequences used by a martial art at or near its inception. They may be traditional sets from the founder's training or created by the founder or early teachers in a specific martial lineage. These forms are usually the core training routines in a system and follow the martial theories of that particular art. Original forms are passed down from generation to generation, continually evolving and adapting with each generation. In many cases, they are the living textbooks of the art.

Borrowed forms are training forms that come from other martial systems. Many martial arts systems borrow training methods (techniques, drills, training sequences, etc.) from older, more established schools/methods. There are several reasons why this happens. Borrowed forms and training methods can increase the number of skills and methodologies in a new or existing system. Adding tried and true skills to a young martial art can increase the general quality of that art in a relatively short amount of time. Older, established forms can be used to understand the orthodox or sometimes original uses of particular skills. These forms are often used as templates for building newer forms and techniques. Adapting older skills for modern

usage is essential to a system's growth. The archaeological method of looking at and researching older methods can help one understand the roots of martial arts much better.

New forms are training routines developed after a system has become established. New forms are usually created for specific training purposes by the system founder or teachers from subsequent generations. This is an ongoing development in all martial arts systems.

FORMS TAUGHT BY DANIEL K. PAI AND THE PAI-LUM ASSOCIATION

In the nineteen sixties, the bulk of the training forms publicly taught by Daniel K. Pai consisted of Okinawan Kata. These were quite possibly Kata learned early in his training. From the mid-sixties until the mid-seventies, training routines that were Pai Family in origin were introduced. It is unknown whether these routines were taught to Daniel K. Pai, created by him, or a combination of the two.

Richmond, VA 1965 -1970

Mr. Warren Cotrell trained with Daniel K. Pai in Richmond, Virginia, during the mid to late 1960s. Mr. Cotrell stated that he was learning a *"...Mixture of Okinawan kempo and Chinese kung-fu. The katas included the basic H patterns, Pinans (1 thru 5), Nahanchi, Bassai Dai, Bassai Sho, Seisan, and Saifa. The self-defenses were influenced by the Chinese style of circular blocking and a lot of open hand techniques... using the palm and wrist for both blocking and striking. He taught me a form that he called Pai-Lum, which included many of the circular hand movements he favored...".*

Form Sequences

Daniel K. Pai lived in Connecticut from 1970 to 1976. During this time frame, he adapted and created many training routines. Of the form sequences created, some were developed to meet the needs of his growing Pai-Lum Association, like Inner Tiger, and others were designed or adapted specifically for individual students.

Bridgeport 1970-1971

According to notes acquired from David L. Smith, some of the training forms on the Bridgeport school syllabus in 1970 were:

1. Pai-Lum

2. Pai-Lim

3. Thousand Step

4. White Crane (Thomas St. Charles' specialty)

5. On-Ji CAN (possibly created for Hilda Kealoha)

6. Crawling Snake (Peter Giarniero's specialty)

7. Golden Fist (brought in by Thomas St. Charles)

8. Mighty Wings (of the eagle?)

9. Sneaky Leopard

10. Hidden Tiger

11. Flamingo

12. Bow & Arrow

13. Speed & Time

Empty hand routines that were developed or showed up in the curriculum during the Hartford years:

1. Three Short Forms of the Tiger

2. Three Fighting Forms of the Tiger

3. Pak-Hou [CAN]

4. Inner Tiger

5. The Tao Form

6. Cau I Chow

7. Ground Crane

8. Mighty Wings of the Eagle

9. Dragon Tail (Taught only to David L. Smith)

10. Dragon Bite

11. Jing Do (two-person)

A large number of forms were also introduced into Pai-Lum by students of Daniel K. Pai. Many of these borrowed form sequences were subsequently adopted, adapted and integrated into the teaching syllabus of the Pai-Lum System. These routines were taught alongside the Pai-based forms and Karate/Kempo Kata in the curriculum; Thomas St. Charles, James Cravens, Dave Everett, Ron Lydestad, Bruce Currie, Patrick McCarthy, and Chris Casey were some of the people responsible for introducing these form sequences into the Pai-Lum system during this period.

Some of the borrowed forms that were brought into the system during the Hartford years (1971-1976) are:

Form Sequences

1. Hung 1

2. Hung 2

3. Young Dragon (Dragon)

4. Snake form

5. Outer Tiger (First half of Tiger-Crane)

6. Crane form (Second half of Tiger-Crane)

7. Flowing form 1 (Liu Chia [WG])

8. Flowing form 2 (Lien Pu [WG])

9. Flowing form 3 (Tuan Ta [WG])

10. Flowing form 4 (Spinning top)

11. Flowing form 5 (Moi Fah [CAN])

12. Taming the Tiger

13. Flowing Water (Bot Bo [CAN])

14. Vital Breath (Tensho [JAP])

15. Chinese Soft Fist

16. Dawn Meditation (Jitte [JAP])

17. Movements of the White Swan (Rohai [JAP])

18. Prance of the Panther (Unsu [JAP])

19. Sun form

20. Cat's play

21. Combat form (Hung-Gar two-person set)

The Florida years 1976 - 1993

Daniel K Pai lived in various locations in Florida from mid 1976 until his passing in 1993. Training forms were continually added or developed by Daniel K. Pai and his senior students. It was during this time frame that most of the T'ai-Chi Ch'üan and T'ai-Chi-like routines were added. Many of the forms developed in Florida were not taught in the Northeast. The exceptions were when Daniel K. Pai taught, or had his students teach them at seminars.

Forms taught in the Northeast during this period are:

1. Inwards Kung-Fu 1 (Short Fist, Ron Lydestad)

2. Inwards Kung-Fu 2 (Straight step, Ron Lydestad)

3. Dragon with Butterfly Hands (Butterfly Hands, Ron Lydestad)

4. One on One (two-person set, Ron Lydestad)

5. Iron Dummy Drills and 5 Pai-based forms (Pai-Lum skills adapted for use on the 18 Bronze-Man training Dummy. Created and introduced by David L. Smith in 1984)

6. Wooden Slide-Dummy training sequences 1-9 (taught by Daniel K. Pai at the White Lotus Kung-Fu Center in Albany, NY, in the Summer of 1985)

7. Dragon Playing with Seven Stars (created by Daniel K. Pai and taught at John Weninger's Li-Lung Kwoon in Windgap, PA. September 1985)

These are not all of the training sequences taught in the many Pai-Lum training halls. Senior Instructors at many training halls developed drills and forms to fill in some voids in their curriculum. Only empty-hand forms have been listed here. Training forms not learned by members

Form Sequences

of the Pai Family Martial Training Association-New York Branch have not been included here. (See Appendix D: Training Form Sequences for a more comprehensive list of training forms)

Forms Used by the Pai Family Martial Training Association

The Pai Family Martial Training Association focuses on five of the earliest training forms attributed to the Pai system. These routines do not contain everything in the system, but there is a continuity of skills in them. Many of the same techniques are used in these sets, usually with a different angle or setup. At the time of their introduction into a teaching syllabus, Daniel K. Pai was between 37 and 43 years old and already a prominent figure in the North American martial arts scene.

Seven of the earliest training forms to publicly come out of the Pai-Lum system are Dragon Dance, Pai-Lum, Pai-Lim, Thousand Step (Chain), On-Ji, Pak-Hau, and White Crane (the form White Crane was only taught to Thomas St. Charles and was not a part of the general curriculum). Of these seven, our branch of the Pai Family art focuses on five: Pai-Lum, Pai-Lim, Thousand Step, On-Ji, and Pak-Hau. The most important being Pai-Lum, Pai-Lim, and Thousand Step.

Table 1: Overlapping techniques and skills found in the earlier Pai Family training sequences

Pai Form Sequence	High to Low Stances	180° to 360° Spin	Jump Kick	Dragon Tail Strikes	Exchange Blocks	Wrist Accel. Strikes	Flanking
Dragon Dance	✔	✔	✔	✔	✔	✔	✔
Pai-Lum	✔	✔	✔	✔	✔	✔	✔
Pai-Lim	✔	✔	✔		✔	✔	✔
Thousand Step	✔	✔	✔	✔	✔	✔	✔
On-Ji	✔	✔	✔		✔	✔	✔
Pa Chow	✔	✔	✔	✔	✔	✔	✔

Early Pai routines:

1. Dragon Dance

2. Pai-Lum (AKA Emperor Dragon)

3. Pai-Lim (AKA Prince Dragon)

4. Thousand Step (Chain)

5. On-Ji   (AKA An Si, Nun's Form, Buddhist Palm, and Hu Hao Lung)

6. Pak-Hau (White Monkey)

7. White Crane (AKA Dance of the White Crane, taught only to Thomas D. St.Charles)

In the Pai-Family Martial Training Association, non-Pai-Lum forms from specific systems, teachers, and lineages were added out of respect. We practice and incorporate theories, skills, drills, forms, and in some cases, martial traditions from teachers that have profoundly impacted our understanding of martial arts.

TABLE 2: CHINESE NAMES AND CHARACTERS FOR SOME OF THE EARLY TRAINING SEQUENCES TAUGHT BY DANIEL K. PAI

Popularly known as	Mandarin	Cantonese	Chinese	English
Dragon Dance	Wu Lung Ch'üan	Mou Lung Kuen	舞龍拳	Dragon Dance
Pai-Lum	Pai Lung Ch'üan	Bak Lung Kuen	白龍拳	White Dragon
Pai-Lim	Pai Lin Ch'üan	Bak Lum Kuen	白林拳	White Forest
Thousand Step	Ch'ien Pu Ch'üan	Chin Bou Kuen	千步拳	Thousand Step
Buddhist Palm	An Si Ch'üan	On Ji Kuen	安寺拳	Peaceful Temple
Pa Chow	Pai Hou Ch'üan	Pak Hau Kuen	白猴拳	White Monkey
White Crane	Pai He Ch'üan	Bok Hok Kuen	白鶴拳	White Crane

Form Sequences

George Dillman and Daniel K. Pai - photo from the mid nineteen sixties.
- From the collection of George Dillman

Chapter Seven

VII FUNDAMENTAL TRAINING:
BASICS

FUNDAMENTAL TRAINING [CHI-BEN KUNG 基本功]

Like any other endeavor, a strong, structurally correct foundation is required to take your art past the novice level of ability or understanding. Foundation training is more than just physical; it also introduces the principles and concepts that all martial arts are built upon.

In Pai-Lum, student levels are traditionally divided into three groups: Beginner, Intermediate, and Advanced. This Chapter will focus on the beginner-level curriculum; fundamental techniques and theories about how they might be used to attack and defend. It will cover terminology, closed fist blocking and striking skills, and basic kicking techniques as taught and practiced in the initial stages of our training. In many Pai-Lum training halls, these skills are referred to as Kempo basics. They are similar to those practiced in Chinese, Okinawan, Japanese, and Hawaiian-based striking arts.

Fundamental techniques, also known as basics, are exaggerated, large-frame exercises meant to train our bodies in specific structures, dynamics, and qualities that help us learn offensive and defensive skills and facilitate future growth in training. They are the first tools a martial arts student learns and the foundation upon which the art is built. An often overlooked part of this training is learning to feel what our bodies are doing.

ABOUT FUNDAMENTAL TRAINING

Standing, stepping, blocking, striking, and kicking are initially practiced in a controlled environment incorporating our martial principles and theories. Precise articulation helps to reduce friction in your movements, allowing for better structure and acceleration; this stage of training is where we learn how to create force (Force equals mass times acceleration). Many repetitions practiced consistently are required for these essential skills to become natural and internalized.

Basic training differs from actual usage in many ways. It is not the most efficient way to execute these skills. However, it is a very efficient way to teach proper structure, coordination, angles of attack, rotational axis, elbow discipline, and martial theories in a principle-based, structured manner.

UPPER BODY SKILLS

Fundamental hand skills (blocking and striking) are initially practiced solo, from a horse stance, with the hand on the opposite side returning to a palm-up, chambered position (at the side of the torso); these are called standing basics. Standing basics are followed by walking basics, structured partner practice, dummy practice (heavy bags, mechanical dummies, etc.), and freestyle training.

WHAT IS A CHAMBER

A chamber is the position an arm or leg is in before and after executing a block, punch, strike, or kick. Chambering is the flexion of an arm or leg into a position from which it can execute a technique; punching, striking, or kicking from a chambered position are extensions.

Two types of chambers are used with arms: The first one, a basic training chamber, is used during the beginning stages of solo and two-person exercises and drills. The second type of chamber is any "on guard" position in which the arms can be held, and techniques can be executed when sparring or defending oneself.

During solo training, most beginner-level hand techniques start from and return to a basic chambered position where the elbow is bent, the fist or palm is in a palm-up position at the side of the torso, and the wrist is at the midline (coronal plane). For our purposes, a chamber is also a position for the non-striking or blocking hand to be drawn to during basic training.

Pulling a hand back to a chamber is initiated with a quick pulling action that becomes a sinking action as the hand is chambered, simultaneously shifting the weight to the chambered side (filling the leg). In solo training, this pulling-back or sinking action is initiated by the dynamics of the opposite arm extending (arm extension, torso rotation, etc.); in actual striking, it is initiated by the recoil from striking/issuing energy into a target.

This training helps to reinforce the core concept of striking opposite the full or filling leg; it also reinforces a concept or action that, in Pai-Lum, is referred to as "technique in, technique out." In application, the withdrawing hand is used to seize, trap, off balance, or root the opponent.

In the Japanese arts, pulling a hand back to a chambered position is called Hikite [JAP] [withdrawing hand, Yin Shou [WG], 引手].

> *"Here the meaning of hikite (pulling hand) is to grab the opponent's arm and pull it, while twisting as much as possible, so that their posture is disrupted."*
>
> *– Gichin Funakoshi, Rentan Goshin Karate Jutsu (1925)*

CENTERLINE

Knowing where you are in relation to your opponent is essential when practicing solo, with a partner, or applying techniques. To understand this, we need to know what a centerline is. A centerline is an imaginary line or axis that runs through the center of an object. When teaching, practicing, and applying techniques, we use three types of centerlines: anatomic centerline, projected centerline, and fight centerline.

An anatomic centerline is an axis, an imaginary line from the crown of our head [pai-hui 百會] down through the center of our torso through the perineum [hui-yin 會陰]. For our purposes, no matter how the torso is positioned, this axis is the anatomic centerline we refer to. When we stand upright, this axis is a vertical line that extends to a point on the floor between our feet, where the sagittal and coronal planes intersect.

A projected centerline is an imaginary line between our anatomic centerline and a focal point outside our torso. When learning and practicing basic blocks or strikes, this focal point is directly in front of us (on the sagittal plane), creating an imaginary line on the front of our torso, separating the left and right halves of our torso. It helps define the area when learning how to articulate techniques.

A fight centerline, or fight line, is a projected centerline between your anatomic centerline and your opponent's anatomic centerline.

TERMINOLOGY AND RULES OF BASIC TRAINING

Strike with the hand opposite the full or filling leg - Striking with the hands or forearms happens on the opposite side of the full or filling leg. This action coincides with a weight shift - one side issues energy as the other receives energy. This weight shift happens rapidly every time there is a strike.

Pull on the same side as the full or filling leg - In all tugging or pulling actions, the line of force is from the attachment (grab or hook) to the elbow (a short range of motion) on the full or filling side of the body. Almost all pulling actions become pushing or sinking actions.

The 90° angle rule - The elbow cannot be less than a ninety-degree angle in basic striking and blocking skills. - When issuing or receiving energy with the forearms and hands (striking, blocking, absorbing), the angle of the (upper) arm and forearm must be greater than 90°. If the elbow is bent less than 90°, it is structurally unstable and prone to collapsing. The exception to this rule is when employing a closing arc or combination closing arc-thrusting technique, such as a slap, inverted hammer-fist, or Boxer-style hook punch to the back or side of an opponent who has moved inside your extended elbow.

LEAD AND REAR

The second version of standing basics has one side of your body closer to the opponent. Lead or lead-side refers to the side of the body closer to the opponent. Rear or rear-side refers to the side of the body farther away from the opponent. For example, if you are in a left fighting stance, your left foot would be your lead foot, and your left hand would be your lead hand, closer to your opponent than your right or rear foot and hand.

Bridge-hands

An essential element of martial arts is Bridge Hands [Ch'iao Shou 橋手].
Our fundamental blocking structures are the first stage of bridge hands training. A bridge is the point of contact between you and your opponent, usually
the forearm or hand. An example would be using your forearm to intercept and
make contact with an opponent's forearm (the bridge) to create an opportunity
to strike or control them (crossing the bridge). Basic blocks, exchange blocks,
and butterfly-hand techniques are traditional skills used in our bridge-hand
training. T'ai-Chi Ch'üan's push-hands, Wing Chun's sticky hands, Southern
Dragon's rubbing arms, and I Liq Chuan's spinning hands are all versions of
bridge-hand training.

Blocking

In Pai-Lum, we define a block as a strike striking a strike. It is an aggressive,
hard-style methodology. We use structure, proper angle, acceleration, and forward intent to intercept, disrupt, and compromise our opponent's attack. Once
contact (the bridge) is made, the goal is to drive through the attack, making
our hands closer to the opponent's body than theirs are to ours. Creating an
advantageous position for us to counter-attack the opponent. Eventually, more
options are available once contact is made.

The four blocks initially taught are:

Inward middle block

Downward or low block

Outward middle block

Upward or high block

Each block should drive forward and cover the solar plexus when practiced
in solo training. These criteria build elbow awareness and help align the blocks
on your projected centerline in solo practice and the fight centerline when applying the technique against a live opponent. All four of these blocks use the
forearm to attack oncoming strikes. Initial contact is made with the muscular
surface of the ventral or dorsal sides of the forearm.

INWARD MIDDLE BLOCK

An inward middle block is a forward and inward strike with the ventral and medial part of the forearm. The inward movement of the block is powered primarily by a rotation of the torso and a slight inward drilling action of the forearm (rotating around the elbow-thumb axis). It should not be practiced or applied by using an inward-swinging action.

As a block, this technique defends the frontal area from the solar plexus to the top of the head. The first 2/3 of this technique is applied against a thrusting type of attack, while the last 1/3 is the finish of the block, driving the striking arm back into the opponent. This block can efficiently block the same side arm (The Left would block a Right strike or vice versa). Once contact is made with the ventral portion of the forearm, this blocking action should drive towards a point just inside the opponent's opposite shoulder, closing and collapsing the opponent's strike. With minor adjustments, this technique can also block thrusting strikes, roundhouse punches, and hook punches from the

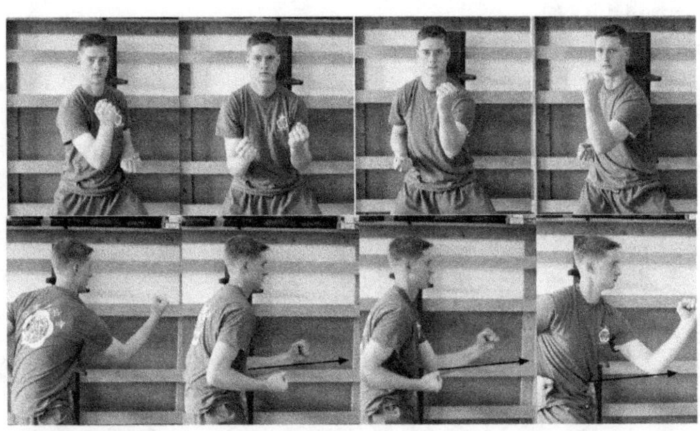

opposite side, though this is not an efficient or safe way to use this block because it leaves your flank wide open.

INWARD MIDDLE BLOCK APPLICATION

Figure 1. The attacker initiates a right punch to the defender's upper torso or head.

Figure 2. The defender initiates a left-handed forward-driving action toward the opponent's center while extending his lead leg.

Figure 3. The defender's forward-driving action intercepts the attacker's punch, making contact with the muscle on the ventral side of his forearm about one fist distance from his wrist, rotating the torso slightly rightward. In many cases, this is enough to block this type of strike effectively.

Figure 4. The defender continues blocking, driving his forearm/elbow towards a point just inside the opponent's opposite shoulder. This often allows the fist of the blocking arm to strike the attacker's face simultaneously.

Figure 1.

Figure 2.

Figure 3.

Figure 4.

Fundamental Training

DOWNWARD OR LOW BLOCK

A basic low block is a forward and downward strike with the forearm. It is initiated with the blocking arm's ax or guillotine-like dropping action. As a block, this technique defends the lower frontal area of the torso from the solar plexus to the Tan-T'ien. The first 2/3 of this technique is applied against a thrusting or rising type of attack. The last 1/3 of this block is driving the attack back into the opponent or defending against a kick.

This technique, with minor adjustments, can block punches or kicks attacking from the side aimed at the lower torso on the same side as the blocking arm.

Inward and downward blocks are related; they start with a forward and inward action. Inward blocks can seamlessly turn into low blocking/attacking actions.

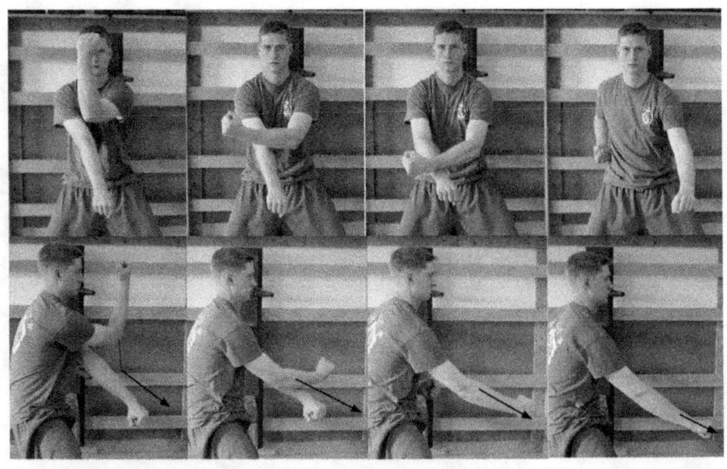

Figure 5. The attacker initiates a left punch to the defender's solar plexus or lower torso.

Figure 6. The defender initiates a left forward-inward-downward dropping action, covering his centerline from the solar plexus downward as he shifts his weight forward

Figure 7. The defender's dropping action intercepts the attacker's punch, making contact with the muscle on the dorsal side of his forearm (about the middle of the forearm) as he steps toward the attacker, continuing to drive forward and downward. In most cases, this is as far as this blocking action needs to go to effectively block a strike from the front.

Figure 8. The defender finishes the block by shifting his weight forward, driving the striking arm back into the attacker. To accomplish this, the defender rotates his forearm around the elbow-thumb axis, driving the medial side of the forearm (the ulna) towards a point 2" behind and 2" below the attacker's Ming-Men.

Figure 5.

Figure 6.

Figure 7.

Figure 8.

Fundamental Training

Outward Middle Block

An outward middle block strikes from the centerline outward. This blocking action is usually initiated with the blocking hand slightly below the level of the attack. It is a Crossing action [Heng 横], which means it strikes from the opposite side of your body. A forward, upward drilling action (rotating around the elbow-pinky axis) that finishes with a forward, palm up, back knuckle action as the blocking side shoulder yields back to a neutral position, absorbing and re-directing the strike.

This technique defends the frontal area from the solar plexus to the top of the head. The first 2/3 of this technique is applied against a thrusting attack. The last 1/3 is either the finish of the block by driving it back into the opponent or, with additional torso rotation, it can be used against a mid or high-level horizontal attack from the same side as the blocking arm.

Outward and high blocks are related in that initial contact is made with the lateral and dorsal sides of the forearm.

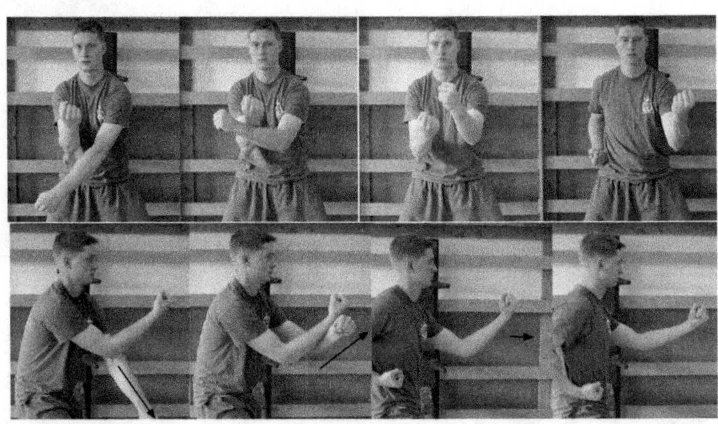

Figure 9. The attacker initiates a right punch to the defender's upper torso or head.

Figure 10. The defender initiates a right-handed forward, upward drilling action covering his centerline from the solar plexus upward.

Figure 11. The defender's drilling action intercepts the attacker's punch, making contact with the muscle on the dorsal side of his forearm about one fist distance from his wrist. The forearm rotates around the elbow-pinky axis, driving a back-fist forward in a drilling/crossing action. In most cases, this is enough to effectively block a strike from the front.

Figure 12. If the attack is still driving forward, the defender finishes the outward block by absorbing and re-directing the strike. Allowing his shoulder to yield back to neutral while driving the dorsal side of his forearm and back-fist forward, driving the attacking arm back into the attacker. This skill requires a combination of T'an-Li (springy energy) and Yao-Li (waist energy). This action can also draw the attacking arm out, over-extending the striking arm and opening the attacker's flank.

Figure 9.

Figure 10.

Figure 11.

Figure 12.

Fundamental Training

UPWARD OR HIGH BLOCK

An upward or high block is a forward and upward strike with the forearm initiated with a drilling action.

As a block, this technique defends the frontal area from the solar plexus to the top of the head. The first 2/3 of this technique is applied against a thrusting attack. The last 1/3 is the finish of the block (by driving it back into the opponent) or a defense against a downward attack. This technique can also block roundhouse and hook punches with minor adjustments by attacking the opponent's forearm at or just below the elbow.

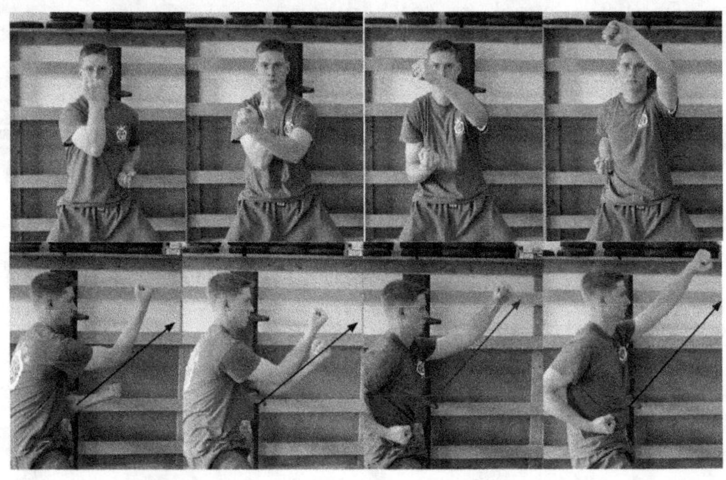

Figure 13. The attacker initiates a left punch to the defender's upper torso or head.

Figure 14. The defender initiates a left-handed drilling action, covering his center-line from the solar plexus upward.

Figure 15. The defender's drilling action intercepts the attacker's punch, making contact with the muscle on the dorsal side of his forearm (on the radius about one fist-distance from his wrist) as he steps toward the attacker. In most cases, this is as far as this blocking action needs to go to effectively block a strike from the front.

Figure 16. This photo shows the defender finishing the block by shifting his weight forward, driving the attacking arm back into the attacker towards a point 2" above and 2" behind the attacker's head.

Figure 13.

Figure 14.

Figure 15.

Figure 16.

Fundamental Training

STRIKING WITH WEAPONS FROM MID-FOREARM TO HAND

(PUNCHING AND STRIKING)

Basic striking skills are divided into thrusting and arcing (opening or closing arc) techniques:

Thrusting strikes are extensions of the arm where the line of force is along the length of the forearm from the center of the elbow through the striking surface. Punches, spear hands, knife hands, and palm strikes are our most prominent thrusting skills.

Opening arc striking skills are extensions of the arm where the striking surface is perpendicular to the length of the striking limb. It is articulated primarily by a contraction of the triceps. Back fists, hammer fists, knife hand strikes, back of the wrist, and forearm strikes are our most prominent opening arc striking skills.

Closing arc striking skills are arm flexions where the striking surface is perpendicular to the length of the striking limb. It is articulated primarily by a contraction of the biceps. Inverted hammer fist, ridge hand, palm, second knuckle, and back-wrist strikes are our most prominent closing arc striking skills.

The first level of strikes that a student learns are punches and arcing strikes utilizing the fist.

PUNCHES

Punches are thrusting actions using fist shapes. The primary striking surface of the fist when punching is the first knuckles (where the bones of the hand and the bones of the fingers meet). In most cases, we strike with the first knuckles of the index and middle fingers. ALL punches are essentially the same; what changes are angles of attack, fist shape, and punching quality.

The differences between straight, uppercut, hook, and roundhouse punches involve different targets and angles of attack. Different fist shapes can be used for specific targets.

PUNCHING QUALITIES

The three qualities employed when punching are Snapping, Point Penetration-Recoil, and Thrusting:

Snapping: Snapping punches issue force at the surface of a target; this is used mainly against hard targets like a person's head. Snapping strikes require an extremely fast strike and withdrawal. Very similar to how a whip strikes.

Point Penetration-Recoil: Point Penetration-Recoil punches strike a target's surface, issuing force deeper into the target. The natural relaxing of the muscles and the force of the opponent's body reacting to the punch (for every action, there is an equal and opposite reaction - Newton's 3rd law of motion) causes the recoil. With proper training, this type of strike can issue force at any depth inside a torso. An example would be striking someone in the chest, displacing the pectoral muscle, issuing force into the ribcage, and the resulting recoil from the punch's impact. In addition, this recoil can be used to initiate other skills and assist strikes with the other side of the body.

Thrust Punch: While all punches are thrusting actions, the context used here is an extreme version of a standard punching action; it could also be called a Full Thrust punch. The Thrust Punches we are talking about here are driven through a target with follow-through. There is no focal point of this type of punch other than through the target!

   Fundamental Training

PALM-UP PUNCH

Palm-up punches are primarily forward, upward-thrusting (uppercut), or drilling actions that strike at or above elbow level, striking vertical or horizontal targets from below.

The four main types of punches where the palm is in an upward-facing position are:

Palm-up punch: A punch that strikes straight forward with the fist in an upward-palm-facing position.

Upset punch: An upset punch strikes forward with an upward impulse after contact.

Uppercut: An uppercut, also known as Cannon punch [Pao-Ch'ui 炮捶], is a type of palm-up punch that strikes upward at horizontal targets from below with a 45° to 90° bend in the arm. A true uppercut is technically closer, articulation-wise, to hook or roundhouse punches in that it strikes from an angle instead of straight forward.

Drilling fist [Tsuan Ch'üan, 鑽拳]: Drilling fist is a punch where the hand moves from a palm-facing-downward to a palm-facing-upward spiral. Most often applied as a true uppercut.

VERTICAL PUNCH

Vertical fist punches are forward, upward, or downward, thrusting actions that can strike vertical or horizontal targets at any level; this is the most used type of punch in Pai-Lum. A variation of vertical punch, called Double Impulse Sun Punch [Jih Ch'üan 日拳], strikes with the first two knuckles (index and middle fingers),' immediately rocking the bottom two knuckles (ring finger and pinkie) upward (while still in contact with the opponent) and forward.

PALM-DOWN PUNCH

Palm-down punches are forward thrusting actions that can strike vertical targets, horizontal targets below elbow level, and specific horizontal targets from below, such as the jaw at any level.

FULL TWIST PUNCH

A classical full-twist front punch articulates three basic punching techniques (palm up, vertical, and palm down) seamlessly linked together in a spiraling action. It is a thrusting technique that starts from a supine or palm-up position,

where the radius and ulna are parallel, the wrist at the midline of the torso and extends into a prone or palm-down extension of the arm, where the ulna crosses over the radius (pronation).

When practicing this technique multiple times during basics practice, alternating arms, the opposite side retracts simultaneously, reversing the process from a palm down to a palm-up position (supination). The elbow stays in the same (downward) position throughout this process, with the forearm rubbing against the torso during the extension and retraction of this technique.

In application, this technique should make contact in the palm-up position, thrusting into the torso as the fist spirals through vertical and palm-down positions (rotating around the elbow-pinkie axis).

HOOK AND ROUNDHOUSE PUNCHES

Hook and roundhouse punches are thrusting strikes that attack the opponent's front quadrant (approximately 45° to 90°). These punches are a combination of arcing and thrusting skills.

A Hook punch combines a closing arc and a thrusting strike toward the opponent's center from an outside line. The range or depth of this technique is from slightly inside to slightly beyond the extended elbow; the fist is palm down or inward depending on the target and depth of the opponent.

ROUNDHOUSE PUNCH

A Roundhouse punch is a slightly higher and deeper version of a hook punch primarily used to strike the head with the palm facing out to allow the proper striking surface to hit the target.

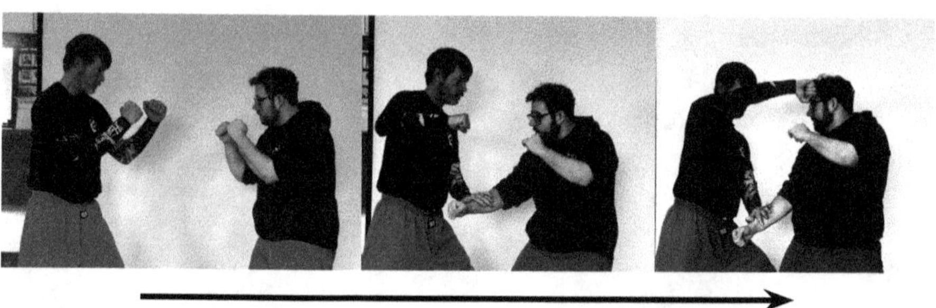

ARCING STRIKES

Arcing strikes are techniques where the line of force is perpendicular to the striking limb. Arcing strikes are divided into opening arc strikes (extensions) and closing arc strikes (flexions).

          Fundamental Training

A Back fist strike is an opening arc technique that combines an arm extension with a driving elbow action. The force of a back fist strike is perpendicular to the length of the striking limb. A back fist can strike downward, outward, and upward. An outward or horizontal back fist strike is a crossing technique, which means that it strikes from the opposite side of the fight centerline. The striking surface is the back of the hand, or extend the wrist and strike with the ridge of the first knuckles (this is called a back-knuckle strike or whipping back knuckle, depending on the quality of the strike.

Kicks

As mentioned in Chapter 4, a kick is a step with a different dynamic. Conversely, any step that cannot become a kick is a poorly executed stepping skill. Kicking skills contain opening arc (snap), closing arc (hook), and thrusting qualities. Kicks also have modifiers such as jumping, flying, and spinning. There are three basic types of kicks: snap, thrust, and hook kicks.

Snap - Thrust - Hook

The primary difference between snap, thrust, and hook kicks is that snap kicks are arcing extensions driven from the front of the hips, thrust kicks are driven from the bottom of the hips, and hook kicks are arcing flexions driven from the back of the hips; the opposite of snap kicks. Initially we focus on snap and thrust kicks.

snap kick articulation
(foot moves to the hip-knee line)

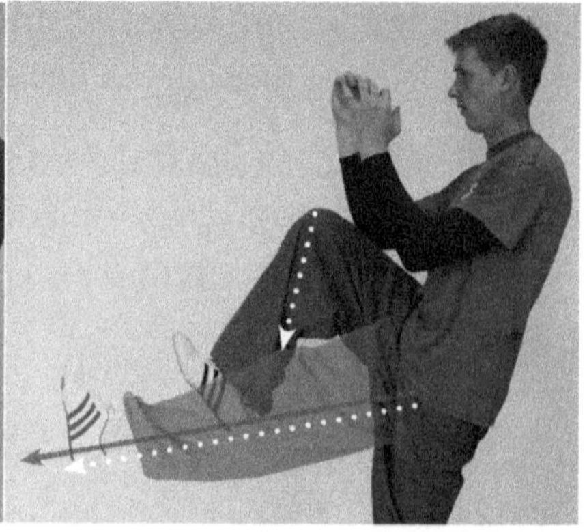

thrust kick articulation
(knee moves to the hip-heel line)

In fundamental training, pure snap, or, thrusting articulations are preferred. In actual usage, qualities are often combined. Two examples are adding a thrusting quality to snap kicks at the point of impact and adding a snapping quality before thrust kicks.

snap kick action

SNAP KICKS

Snap kicks are leg extensions that strike in an arc. All front snap kicks start with the front of the thigh driving forward (toward the target), followed by the shin and foot. It is an extension with the line of force perpendicular to the front of the lower leg. In snap kicks, the striking surfaces (shin, instep, toes, or ball of the foot) move to the hip-knee line during extension.

Snap kicks strike upward (front snap kicks, side snap kicks), targeting horizontal and angular targets from below or inward (Round-house kicks), striking the front quadrant of the opponent from about 45 to 90 degrees from the side.

FRONT SNAP KICK

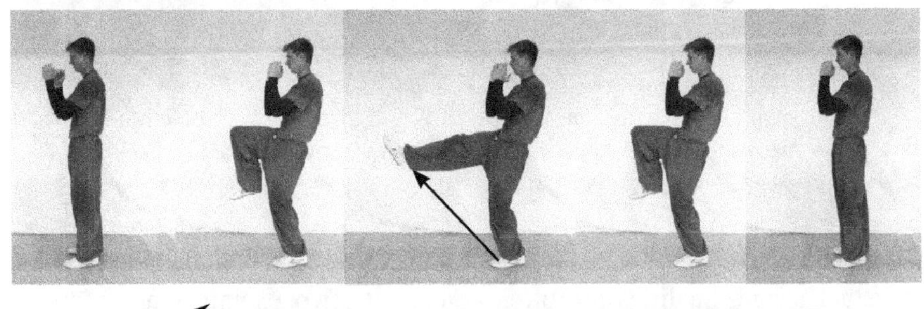

A front snap kick is an arcing extension in the direction the front of the thigh is pointing. This kick strikes in a forward and upward arc, striking with the ball of the foot, toes, instep, or shin.

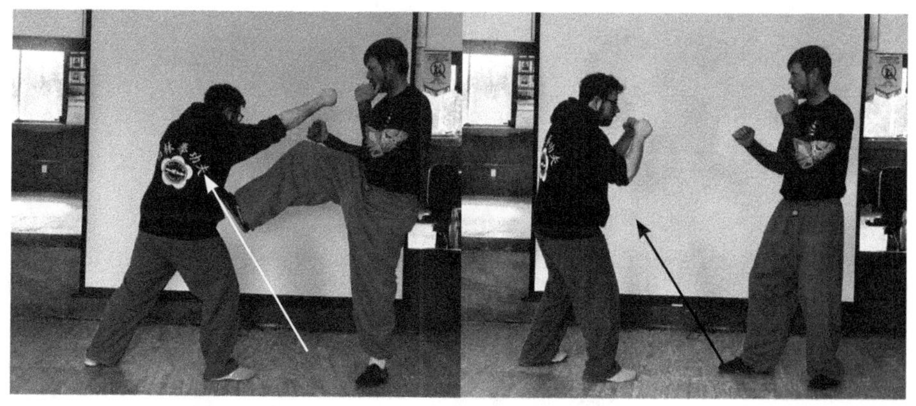

Roundhouse Kick

A roundhouse kick is an arcing extension in which the kicking leg starts with the thigh driving forward, then, with an inward rotation of the body, while pivoting on the ball of the foot of the base leg, drives the front of the thigh inward. This kick strikes the front quadrant somewhere between 45° and 90° from the side, striking with the ball of the foot, toes, instep, or shin.

Thrust kicks are leg extensions that strike using the principle of push. In thrust kicks, the knee moves to the hip-foot line during extension.

To execute a thrusting action, lift one knee as high as possible in front of you, the lower leg hanging, perpendicular to the ground. Stomp downward with your foot landing in the same spot it started, the line of force being a straight line from the center of the knee through the length of the Fibula and the striking surface (bottom, blade edge, heel, or ball of the foot). This pure thrusting action drives the leg from the bottom of the hips; all thrust kicks have this quality. This action is a downward thrust or stomp kick. If you do this action with your hips curled forward, it is a front thrust kick; curl the hips backward for a back thrust kick, and curl the hips to the side for side thrust kicks. Thrust kicks strike vertical targets with the bottom of the foot, blade edge, heel, or ball. Stomp kicks are low-thrust kicks that can strike the top of horizontal and vertical targets.

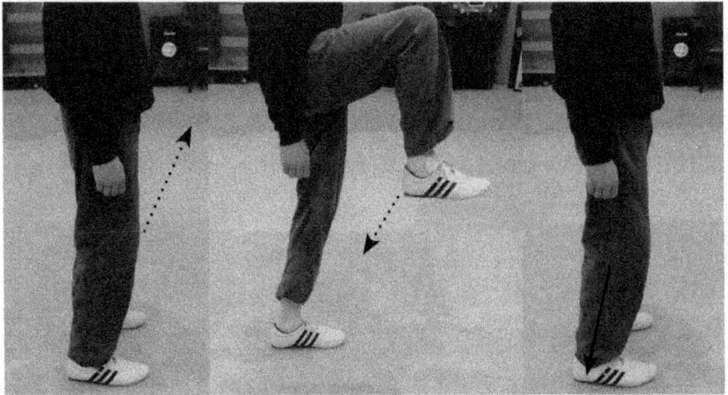

thrust kick action

A front thrust kick is a leg extension, using the principle of push, in the direction the front of the thigh is pointing; the hip needs to be curled forward to allow the kick to be issued from the bottom of the hip. This kick strikes with the ball of the foot, toes, blade edge, sole, or heel.

A back kick is a leg extension, using the principle of push, in the direction the back of the thigh is pointing; the back of the kicking side hip has to be curled so the kick can be issued from the bottom of the hip. This kick strikes primarily with the heel, though the blade edge or sole may also be used.

A Side thrust kick is a leg extension, using the principle of push, in the direction the outside or lateral side of the thigh is pointing; this requires the kicking side hip to be curled to the side to enable the kick to be issued from the bottom of the hip. This kick strikes with the blade edge, heel, or sole.

     Fundamental Training

Hook Kicks

Hook kicks are leg flexions that strike in an arc, the opposite of snap kicks. The line of force is perpendicular to the back of the lower leg. The striking surfaces of a hook kick are the back of the calf, the back of the heel, or the bottom of the foot. Hooking-type kicks require the striking surface of the kick to be beyond the target because the strike happens during flexion. Sickle kicks are low, inward hook kicks.

Crescent Kicks

Crescent Kicks are arcing front thrust kicks with a closing or opening of the Kua, creating the arcing dynamic during the kick. Inside or inward, Crescent kicks strike from an outside line inward. Outside or outward, Crescent kicks strike from an inside line outward. Both inward and outward Crescent kicks are initiated with a snap-kicking action with a slight opening (inward Crescent kick) or closing (outward Crescent kick) of the Kua, a thrust-kicking action with a closing (inward Crescent kick) or opening (outward Crescent kick) of the Kua followed by a sickle, or hooking type action on the retraction. The striking surface for inside Crescent kicks is the foot sole; outside Crescent kicks strike with the blade edge of the foot or the outside of the calf.

Pai-Lum has always been taught in English, with Chinese, Japanese, and Hawaiian phrases added for specific things. Since the mid-nineteen sixties, the Chinese language used in Daniel K. Pai's martial teachings used different dialects and systems of romanization.

In the early nineteen seventies, Chinese was used for counting, names of basic techniques, and form sequences. Most of the Chinese terminology that was, and still is, used in many training halls was from the Mandarin dialect.

CLASS TERMINOLOGY

Some key terms that could be used during class time are:

Commands:	Wade-Giles	Chinese	Pinyin
Line up	p'ai tui	排隊	paidui
Break	li cheng	立正	lizheng
Stand up	ch'i li	起立	qili
Begin	k'ai shih	開始	kaishi
Stop	t'ing	停	ting
Sit	tso hsia	坐下	zuoxia
Ready	yu pei	預備	yubei
Salutation	hsing li	行禮	xingli
Thank you	hsieh hsieh	謝謝	xiexie
Many thanks	to hsieh	多謝	duoxie
See you again	tsai chien	再見	zaijian

Counting:	Wade-Giles	Chinese	Pinyin
1	i	一	yi
2	er	二	er
3	san	三	sān
4	ssu	四	sì
5	wu	五	wu
6	liu	六	liu
7	ch'i	七	qī
8	pa	八	ba
9	chiu	九	jiu
10	shih	十	shi

It should be noted that the number four is very unlucky in Chinese culture. The number 4 [si 四] sounds like the word for death [si 死]; therefore, a name with four characters is not thought to be good. It would typically be shortened to three characters or lengthened to five. That is why system names tend to end with Ch'üan [fist 拳] instead of Ch'üan-fa [fist method or boxing 拳法], or Ch'üan-shu [fist method or boxing 拳術]. This is the reason Pai-Lung Ch'üan, or Pai-Te Lung Ch'üan-Fa are often used in place of Pai-Lung Ch'üan-Fa.

Appendix B: Martial Titles, Terms of Address, and English titles

Wade-Giles[WG], Pinyin[PY], Yale[Y], Cantonese[CAN]

Instructor/Teacher Terms of Address

Elder Teacher:
老師. Lao-Shih[WG], Laoshi[PY], Lau-Shr[Y], Losi[CAN]
A term used for a teacher-level practitioner over 50 years old.

High (level) Teacher:
杲師, Kao-Shih[WG], Gaoshi[PY], Gau-Shr[Y], Gousi[CAN]
A term used for a teacher-level practitioner over 40 years old.

Teacher's Teacher:
師公, Shih-Kung[WG], Shigong[PY], Shr-Gung[Y], Si-gung[CAN]
A term used for your teacher's teacher.

Teacher- Instructor:
師傅 Shih-Fu[WG], Shifu[PY], Shr-fu[Y], Sifu[CAN]
A general term for teacher. It is a homophone with 師父 (Teacher Father).

Instructor:
教練 Chiao-Lien[WG], Jiaolian[PY], Jyau-Lyan[Y], Gau Lin[CAN]
A term used for instructor, sports coach, trainer.

Honorific Terms

Ancestor/Grandfather Teacher:
祖師, Tsu-Shih[WG], Zu shi[PY], Dzu Shr[Y], Sijo[CAN]
Ancestor teacher or Grandfather teacher. A term used for the founder of a
martial system.

Ancestor Teacher Grandfather:
祖師爺, Tsu Shih-I[WG], Zushiye[PY], Dzu Shr-Ye[Y]
Essentially the same as Ancestor/Grandfather Teacher.

Ancestor Teacher:

宗師, Tsung-Shih[WG], Zongshi[PY], Dzung-Shr[Y], Jung Si[CAN]

Can be used as a term for Grandmaster, literally Ancestor or lineage teacher.

Teacher Father:

師父, Shih-Fu[WG], Shifu[PY], Shr-Fu[Y], Sifu[CAN]

A term used for a male lineage teacher by his disciples. It is a homophone with 師傅 (Teacher instructor).

Teacher Mother:

師母, Shih-Mu[WG], Shimu[PY], Shr-Mu[Y], Simo[CAN]

A term traditionally used for the wife of a lineage teacher. In modern times it is also used for a female lineage teacher by her disciples.

Uncle (teacher's older brother):

師伯, Shih-Po[WG], Shibo[PY], Shr-Bwo[Y], Sibok[CAN]

A term used for your teacher's senior male classmate.

Uncle (teacher's younger brother):

師叔, Shih-Hsu[WG], Shishu[PY], Shr-Shu[Y], Sisuk[CAN]

A term used for your teacher's junior male classmate.

Aunt (teacher's sister):

師姑, Shih-Ku[WG], Shigu[PY], Shr-Gu[Y], Sigu[CAN]

A term used for your teacher's female classmate.

Elder Brother:

師兄, Shih-Hsiung[WG], Shixiong[PY], Shr-Syung[Y], Sihing[CAN]

A term used for your senior male classmate.

Elder Sister:

師姐 Shih-Chieh[WG], Shijie[PY], Shr-Jye[Y], Sije[CAN]

A term used for your senior female classmate.

Younger Brother:

弟 Shih-Ti[WG], Shidi[PY], Shr-Di[Y], Sidi[CAN]

A term used for your Junior male classmate.

Younger Sister:

師妹 Shih-Mei[WG], Shimei[PY], Shr-Mei[Y], Simui[CAN]

A term used for your junior female classmate.

<u>**ENGLISH TITLES: GRANDMASTER, MASTER, DISCIPLE, STUDENT**</u>

Grandmaster:

The term "Grandmaster," in most martial art methods, refers to the head person in a particular martial system, the inheritor or gatekeeper of a particular method. To be considered a Grandmaster, one would have to be designated a system inheritor (which may be more than one person) by the previous Grandmaster and inherit the position when the current Grandmaster passes away. In addition, one could use the title Grandmaster when one creates a new system or is the head of a branch system. The Grandmaster is responsible for everything concerning their martial system. The Grandmaster should be the primary source of knowledge in their particular system.

Master:

The term "Master" for our uses here is defined as "a skilled practitioner of a particular art," an authority or expert in a particular method. A master is also considered a senior-level teacher. The closest Chinese equivalent is Shih [師] which means teacher, master, or specialist. When Shih is combined with Fu [傅], it means teacher-instructor. Other terms attributed to master-level practitioners are Lao-Shih [老師] and Kao-Shih [高師], elder teacher and high (level) teacher, respectively. Master-level practitioners are also disciples of their Teacher and are responsible for their specific art's quality, teaching, and perpetuation.

Disciple:

A follower or student of a teacher, leader, or philosopher. One who accepts and assists in spreading a school's or an individual's teachings. In Chinese martial arts, one becomes a disciple when they are accepted as a formal/personal student of a Shih-Fu, [師傅 teacher-instructor]. Accepting a personal student is a very formal event, usually requiring a discipleship ceremony called Pai Shih [拜師 bow to the teacher]. After the ceremony, the relationship is defined in a familial context, and the usage of Shih-Fu becomes teacher-father [師父] or teacher-mother [師母 Shih-Mu]. The disciple's job is to learn the entire art they train in and make sure it passes on to the next generation.

Disciples are inner circle students. There are two standard terms for disciple in Chinese; disciple-apprentice [徒弟, T'u-Ti[WG], Tou Dai[CAN]] or disciple-follower [弟子, Tì Tzu[WG], Dai Gee[CAN]]. Listed below are categories of disciples.

Inside the Door Disciple:

入門弟子, Ju Men Ti Tzu[WG], Yap Moon Dai Gee[CAN]].

The first stage of discipleship. Accepted as a lineage-holding personal student of an earlier generation, inside the room disciple, or higher. Though there is no "set in stone" time frame for a student to petition to become a disciple, it usually happens when they attain their first higher level. On rare occasions, it could happen at 1st Lower level.

Inside the Room Disciple:

入室弟子, Ju Shih Ti Tzu[WG], Yap Sut Dai Gee[CAN].

The second stage of discipleship. Accepted as a lineage-holding, personal student of an earlier generation head of school or system. You must be a teacher-level, Inside the Door Disciple, to be considered. An Inside the room disciple is allowed to accept personal students and use the school or system name without restrictions. More than likely, a system inheritor.

Adopted Grandchildren:

Being a disciple is very similar to being adopted. In the late nineteen seventies, Grandmaster Daniel K. Pai decided that his closest disciples would be officially known as "Adopted Grandchildren," this was and is unique to the Pai Family system. The Pai Family Martial Training Association believes this was a special bond between Grandmaster Pai and his second-generation senior students. Since Dr. Pai's passing, the Pai Family Martial Training Association has reverted to the traditional use of disciple for all subsequent generations.

Student:

Technically, we are all students, but for our purposes here in defining our hierarchy, the term Student is used to define the General Members of our training halls. These members are considered "Outer Circle Students," Those who have not yet been accepted as Family members. This group, as well as being novices in our art, are also the most important members. These are the bulk of the people attending classes at a training hall; their job is to train. They spend their entire time learning and perfecting the fundamentals of our art.

While most students can become competent in their art and benefit significantly from their training, only a small percentage of this group become highly skilled Practitioners, Disciples, and Teachers.

JAPANESE TITLES:

JAPANESE	MANDARIN CHINESE		MINIMUM RANK CRITERIA

Teacher or Instructor:
Sensei   (Xiansheng)   先生

Polished Instructor:
Renshi   (Lianshi)   錬士   4th Dan and above

Senior Teacher or Expert :
Kyoshi   (Jiaoshi)   教士   6th Dan and above

Teacher of Teachers:
Hanshi   (Fanshi)   範士   8th Dan and above

Chief Instructor:
Shihan   (Shifan)   師範

Head of Family or System:
Soke   (Zongjia)   宗家

APPENDIX C: CREEDS AND CODES OF THE PAI FAMILY ARTS

THE WHITE DRAGON PLEDGE

To serve people with good manners
To serve elders with honor and respect
Will not use violence
Try to achieve the ultimate goal of God and the sages
To remember always the true meaning of humility and good character
And to uphold and protect the spirit of the warrior

DRAGON CREED

I am what I am because I choose to be. I am a Dragon by choice and am subject to its laws. My brothers and sisters are my heart and my mind. Even though we may disagree with each other we still strive to be one, forgetting all categories and letting energy which wishes to exist, exist. But as a Dragon, I must go forth to seek the Tao and the void, understanding myself and finding peace within.

WARRIOR'S CODE

The warrior is a man/woman who dedicates his/her life to the cause which made him/her what he/she is. What governs the warrior is the foresight that he/she has to see beyond the present and into the future, beyond the capabilities of those who follow him/her. The warrior is dedicated to defend the Honor, the Creed, the Pride, and the Self-Respect for what he/she wishes to be called ... Dragon, Dragon, Dragon. Wisdom, Courage, Honor, Strength, Purity, all Knowledge.

THE PRAYER OF MASTER CHING

Though struggling through the veil of ignorance I place faith in the precious protectors of the law. Knowing that my heart will forever change, I vow to perfect understanding of the great way. Fearlessness of Death and Life is the double edged sword of enlightenment which I shall carry. Respect to all, Trust in the Way, and service to the teachers are the doors to the path, all else is wasteful. Those of caution fear and doubt, need not enter within this great secret road, for it is strewn with the bones of those who could not defeat the Dragons of desire and wastefulness. Therefore O Wise Ones, I pray that you guide me and direct me upon the path to attainment which I hereby promise to observe and follow faithfully. In the union of the ten directions and the void-ness of idea lie expression and wisdom, I vow to attain them.

                                        Appendix C

Training Sequences that have been learned and trained in the NY branch of the Pai Family Martial Training Association over the years. (including the White Lotus Kung-Fu Center, the White Dragon Kung-fu Center, The Kung-Fu Center, and Ying-Hao Wu-Kung Kuan)

PAI-LUM

(Early Pai, borrowed and Pai created form sequences)

Stance Exercise #1 [PL]

Elbow Sequence exercise [PL]

Blocking drill #1 [PL, PSK]

Dragon exercise [PL]

Short form of the tiger [PL]

Movements of the tiger [PL]

Twist of the tiger [PL]

3 fighting forms of the tiger [COK PL]

Hung 1 [HK PL]

Hung 2 [HK, PL]

Young dragon [SFA, PL]

Dragon bite [PL]

Chinese soft fist [PL COK]

Flowing form 1 *(Liu chia)* [HNGK PL]

Flowing form 2 *(Lien pu)* [NF PL]

Flowing form 3 *(Tuan Ta)* [NF PL]

Flowing form 4 *(Spinning top)* [PL NF]

Flowing form 5 *(Moi Fah)* [CLF PL]

Outer tiger [HNGK SFA PL]

Taming the tiger [HNGK PL]

Golden fist [COK PL]

Crawling snake [PL]

Flowing water [PL NF]

Vital breath *(Tensho)* [COK PL]

Pounce of the panther *(Unsu)* [COK PL]

Movements of the white swan *(Rohai)* [COK PL]

Dawn meditation *(Jitte)* [COK PL]

Cat's play [COK PL]

Sun form [PL]

Snake form [SFA PL]

SYSTEM NAME ABBREVIATIONS	
COK	- Chinese/Okinawan Kempo
PL	- Pai-Lum
NF	- Northern Fist
SF	- Southern Fist
PSK	- Pai Shou Kempo
NPM	- Northern Praying Mantis
TSP	- T'ien Shan P'ai
WC	- White Crane
HNGK	- Hung-Ga Kuen (LSW)
HK	- Hung-Kuen (village)
CLF	- Choy Li Fut
SFA	- Shaolin five Animal System
SLH	- Southern Lohan
PKC	- Pa-Kua Chang
TCC	- T'ai-Chi Ch'uan
HIC	- Hsing-I Ch'uan
HPGK	- Hop-Ga Kuen
FGK	- Fut-Ga Kuen
GE	- Golden Eagle
SNT	- Shorin No Tora

Inwards kung fu *(originally known as Short Fist)* SF PL
Inwards kung fu 2 *(originally known as Straight Step)* SF PL
Dragon with butterfly hands *(originally known as Butterfly hands)* SF PL
Dragon dance PL
Pai lum *(Pai-Lung Ch'uan)* PL
Pai lim *(Pai-Lin Ch'uan)* PL
Pa Chow *(Pak Hau Kuen)* PL
Thousand step PL
On-Ji *(An Ssu, Hu, hao, lung Ch'uan)* PL
White crane *** *(Thomas St. Charles only)* PL
Lung Wei ch'uan*** *(Dragon's tail , David L. Smith only)* PL
Inner tiger PL
Mighty wings of the eagle PL
Dragon playing with seven stars PL
One on one PL
Tiger-Crane two person routine *(Thomas St. Charles)* PL
Jing do PL
Combat form *(Hung ch'uan tuei ta)* HNGK PL
Pai Lum Slide Dummy Forms 1-6 PL
Kwan tao PL HNGK
Hu wei ta tao *(Tiger Tail Broadsword)* CLF PL

PAI-SHOU KEMPO
(Drills, exercises and forms created by David L.Smith)
 5 Star Horse - stance ex. PSK
 Kempo 1 PSK
 Kempo 2 PSK
 Kempo 3 PSK
 Punch/grab hand articulation form
 (From Pai-Lum drills) PSK PL
 Triangle steps PSK
 13 point stick PSK
 13 point saber PSK
 5 star staff PSK
 5 star saber PSK
 Intermediate staff PSK
 Chang Mei Kun PSK
ADDITIONAL SETS
 Tan-Tui 1-4 NF

Kung-li ch'uan [NF]
Beng bu [NPM]
San t'sai chien [NF]
Northern saber [NF]
Chinese animal sequence ex. [NF SF]
Shr san shou *(Seisan)* [COK SF]

TAIWAN BASED FORMS

Nan Shaolin Shih-Pa T'eng -Jen fa
(South Shaolin 18 Bronzeman method)   *- Ch'en Chin-Yuan* 陳金源
    Chuan shou - chuan shen
    Pai Drills - *(Pai Method developed by David L. Smith)*
    Ch'en Drills
    New forms (Pai) 1-5 - *(Pai Method developed by David L. Smith)*
    Old forms (Ch'en) 1-5

T'ung-I T'ang Wu-Yi
(Village Hung style, T'ien-Shan P'ai, Ch'in-Na)   *- Hsieh Hsin-Keng* 謝辛庚
    Mei hua tao er lu
    Hung's hsiao he hsing (small crane)
    Kwan tao (Taiwan)
    Kwan tao (lion dance set)
    Smoking stick
    36 Ch'in-na
    Three section staff vs. spear

Feeding Crane, Golden Eagle   *- Ma Tsao-Jih* 馬朝日
    San tei ch'uan
    Angle Fist

Southern Lohan   *- Wang Tsao-Yang* 王朝陽
    San chi ch'uan
    Lohan #8
    Double axe

Hop-Ga Kuen, Bak Hok Pai   *- Steven Nacua*
   Luk Lik Kuen
   Kau Da Kuen
   Hop-Ga Kuen 1
Praying Mantis   *- Patrick Hodges*
   Drunken Luohan
Fut-Ga Kuen
   Spirit Fist
Northern Long Fist   *- Kwan Sai-Hung*
   Shih-Lu Tan-Tui 1 - 10
T'ai-Chi ch'uan
   24 form
   Yang style long form
   T'ai chi chien
   T'ai chi tao
Hsing-I Ch'uan
   Five fists
   Twelve animals
Pa-Kua Chang
   Cheng Ting-Hua Eight mother palms
   Cheng Ting-Hua Eight palms
   Chiang Rong-Chiao – Original form
White Crane   *- Dr. Yang Jwing-Ming*
   Two person blocking set
   (up and down limbs)
Hsing-I Ch'uan   *- Liang Shou-Yu*
   Five fists
   Wu hsing lien huan ch'uan *(Linking set)*
   Hsing-i ch'uan
   En hsin pao *(two person set)*
Pa-Kua Chang
   Eight Palms-Dragon shape Pa Kua
Kobudo   *- Vince Ward*
   Nunchaku Kata
   Sai Kata

Arrington, George
Danzan Ryu Essentials: A Sourcebook from the Danzan-Ryu Jujutsu Homepage and MORE!
CreateSpace Independent Publishing Platform, 2011. 170 p

Bergin, Billy
Loyal to the Land: The Legendary Parker Ranch, 750-1950
University of Hawaii Press, 2003. 368 p

Bergin, Billy
Loyal to the Land: The Legendary Parker Ranch, 1950-1970 Volume 2
University of Hawaii Press, 2015. 336 p

Bishop, John
Kajukenbo:The Original Mixed Martial Art
Vermont: C.E.Tuttle, 2006. 222p

Bishop, Mark
Okinawan Karate: teachers, styles and secret techniques
ColliervilleTN: Instant Publisher.com, 1999. 176p

Cheng Man-Ch'ing & Smith, Robert W.
T' ai-Chi: the "Supreme Ultimate" exercise for health, sport & self defense
Vermont: C.E.Tuttle, 1967. 112p

Cheong Cheng Leong & Dreager, Donn F.
Phoenix Eye Fist: A Shaolin fighting art of south China
New York: Weatherhill, 1977. 170p

Chin, Sam F.S.
I Liq Chuan - Martial Art of Awareness
Mount. Kisco, New York: Chin Family I Liq Chuan Association, 2006. 124p

Chin, Sam F.S.
System guide 3rd edition- Martial Art of Awareness
Mount. Kisco, New York: Chin Family I Liq Chuan Association, 2019. 183p

Chinese Historical Society of America
The Hawai'i Chinese: History & Perspectives – The Journal of the Chinese Historical Society of America, chsa.org
San Francisco, California, 2010. 158 p

Chow, David & Sprangler, Richard.
Kung Fu: History, philosophy & technique
California: Unique publications, 1980. 220p

Chun, William Q.C. Jr
Goshin Jitsu Kenpo / Chinese Kempo Kai
Fairfield California: Goshin Jitsu Kenpo / Chinese Kempo Kai publishing, 2020. 353p

Cravens, James
The Boxing
Chinese Boxing Institute International
Ft. Lauderdale, FL, 1998. 236p

Dao Deng-Ming
Chronicles of Tao
New York: Harper One, 1993. 496p

Dillman, George A.
Prometheus: The George Dillman Story
Kalindi Press, 2013, 304p

Dreager, Donn F. & Smith, Robert W.
Comprehensive Asian Fighting Arts
New York: Kodansha, 1969. 207p

Glick, Clarence E..
Sojourners and Settlers: Chinese Migraants in Hawaii
Hawaii Chinese History Center and thr University Press of Hawaii, 1980, 394p

Hawaiian Historical Society
Hawaiian Journal of History, Volume 08
Chinese Merchant-Adventurers and Sugar Masters in The Hawai'i:1802-1852
Honolulu: Hawaiian Historical Society, 1974

Henning, Stanley E.
Academia Encounters the Chinese Martial Arts
China Review International, FALL 1999. Vol. 6, No. 2
University of Hawaii Press

Henning, Stanley E. (Compiled by Michael A. DeMarco, M.A.)
Henning's scholarly works on Chinese Combative Traditions
Via Media Publishing, 2018. 142p

Henning, Stanley E.
The Chinese Martial Arts in Historical Perspective
Military Affairs, Dec. 1981, Vol. 45, No. 4 (Dec. 1981). pp. 173-179

Hong Ze-Han, Translated by Christopher Bates
Blurred Boundries: A Martial Arts Legacy and the shaping of Taiwan
Wolfboro, NH: YMAA Publication Center, 2023. 532p

Hsu, Adam
Life Is Too Short For Bad Kung Fu
California: Plum Publications, 2019. 223p

Hsu, Adam
The Sword Polisher's Record - The Way of Kung-fu
Vermont: Tuttle Publishing, 1998. 208p

Jou Tsung-Hua
The Tao of Tai-Chi Chuan
NY: tai-chi foundation, 1981. 271p

Khim P'ng Chye & Dreager, Donn F.
Shaolin: An introduction to Lohan fighting techniques
Vermont: C.E.Tuttle, 1979. 169p

Kim, Richard
The Weaponless Warriors
California: Ohara Publications, 1974. 112p

Kiong Tjoa Khek & Dreager, Donn F.
Shantung Black Tiger: A Shaolin fighting art of north China
New York: Weatherhill, 1976. 149p

Lee Kam Wing
The Secret of the Seven Star Mantis Style
Hong Kong: Lee Kam Wing Martial Art Sports Assoc., 1985. 234p

Lee Ying Arng
The Secret Arts of Chinese Leg Manoeveres in Pictures
Hong Kong: Sin Poh Amalgamated, 1972. 114p

Liang Shou Yu, Yang Jwing Ming, and Wen Ching-Wu
Baguazhang: Theory and applications
Massachusetts: YMAA, 1994. 364p

Liang Shou Yu & Yang Jwing Ming
Hsing Yi Chuan: Theory and applications
Massachusetts: YMAA, 1990. 221p

Lin Meimei, Xie Tinghui
A generation of martial arts master Luo Ganzhang: Master Aqian, the ancestor of Tongyi Hall and his martial arts inheritance
Taiwan: Wunan Book Publishing Co., Ltd. 2007. 424p

Louie, Emma Woo.
Chinese American Names: Tradition& Transition
North Carolina: McFarland & Company Inc., 2008. 230p

Mattson, George E.
Uechi Ryu Karate Do : Classical Chinese Okinawan self defense
New Hampshire: Peabody Publishing Co., 1974. 492p

McCarthy, Patrick
The Bible of Karate: Bubishi
Charles E. Tuttle, 1995. 492p

McCarthy, Patrick
Classical Kata of Okinawan Karate
Black Belt Communications, Incorporated, 1987. 256p

McCarthy, Patrick
Legend of the Fist
Createspace Independent Publishing Platform, 2018. 334p

Nagaboshi, Tomio (Terrance Dukes)
Mushindo Karate Do Training Manual
United Kingdom: Mushindo Honbu, 1971. 237p

Nishiyama, Hiditaka & Brown, Richard C.
Karate: The art of empty hand fighting
Vermont: C.E.Tuttle, 1959. 251p

Nordyke, Elenor C., and Lee, Richard K. C.
The Chinese in Hawai'i: A Historical and Demographic PerspectiveSan Francisco,
The Hawaiian Journal of History, Vol. 23 1989. 31p

O'Connor, Greg
Aikido Student Handbook
California: Frog, LTD., 1993. 108p

Oyama, Masutatsu
This is Karate: revised edition
Japan: Japan Publications Inc., 1965. 368p

Parker, Ed
Secrets of Chinese Karate
New Jersey: Prentice-Hall Inc., 1963. 239p

Pickands, Marcia L.
The Psychic Self-Defense Personal Training Manual
Weiser Books, April 1997. 128 p

Martin Pickands
Dragon Tales
Updated in 1998 and 2009 by Marcia L. Pickands
Anthropology Department
State University of New York at Albany, 1979. 20 p

Shahar, Meir
Ming-Period Evidence of Shaolin Martial Practice
Harvard Journal of Asiatic Studies, Dec. 2001, Vol. 61, No. 2
 Harvard-Yenching Institute

Smith, Robert W.
Chinese Boxing: Masters and Methods
New York: Kodansha, 1974. 112p

Smith, Robert W.
Hsing I: Chinese mind-body Boxing
New York: Kodansha, 1974. 112p

Smith, Robert W.
Pa Kua: Chinese Boxing for fitness & self defense
New York: Kodansha, 1967. 160p

Smith, Robert W.
Secrets of Shaolin Temple Boxing
Vermont: C.E.Tuttle, 1964. 71p

Sun Lu-Tang (translated by Albert Liu, edited by Dan Miller)
Xing Yi Quan Shu: The study of form-mind Boxing
California: Unique Publications, 2000. 312p

Takacs, Jeff
A Case of Contagious Legitimacy: Kinship, Ritual, and Manipulation in Chinese Martial Arts Societies
Cambridge University Press, Modern Asian Studies, Oct. 2003, Vol. 37, No. 4, pp. 885-917

Thalken, Jason, PhD
Fight like a Physicist
Wolfboro, NH: YMAA Publication Center, 2015. 157p

Theriault, Jean Yves
Full Contact Karate
Chicago: Contemporary Books Inc., 1983. 214p

Tong Zhongyi (translated by Tim Cartmell)
The Method of Chinese Wrestling
California: North Atlantic Books, 2005. 229p

Un, H.B.
Pak Mei Kung Fu: White Eyebrow
London: Paul Crompton, 1974. 81p

Un, H.B.
Praying Mantis Kung Fu
London: Paul Crompton, 1973. 84p

Un, H.B.
Gung Lik Kune : Kung fu manual
London: Paul Crompton, 1978. 46p

Yang, Jwing Ming & Bolt, Jeffery A.
Shaolin Long fist Kung Fu
California: Unique Publications, 1981. 248p

Yang Jwing Ming
Shaolin Chin Na: The seizing art of kung fu
California: Unique Publications, 1982. 159p

Yang Jwing Ming
Analysis of Shaolin Chin Na: Instructors manual for all martial arts
Massachusetts: YMAA, 1987. 196p

Wile, Douglas
T' ai-Chi Touchstones: Yang Family Secret transmissions
New York: Sweet Chi Press, 1983. 160p

Wong, James I.
A Source Book in the Chinese Martial Arts: History, philosophy, systems & styles
California: Koinonia Publications, 1978. 140p

Wong Kiew Kit
Introduction to Shaolin Kung Fu
Colorado: Paladin Press, 1981. 86p

Zhuang Jiaren (Research Assistant)
A special study on the development history of local martial arts in Taiwan-Phase II research results report
Taiwan, ROC: National Institute of Physical Education, 1992. 124p

Additional material has been attained from the following sources:

International Ryukyu Karate Research Society
https://www.koryu-uchinadi.com

Brennan Translations: Translations of Chinese martial arts manuals
https://brennantranslation.wordpress.com/

Newspapers.com
Newspaper Archive.com
Reading Eagle (PA)
Richmond Times-Dispatch (VA) Archives
Google News Archive

Hours of conversations, phone calls, emails, texts, and classes with David L. Smith, Marcia Pickands, Steven Nacua, Thomas D. St. Charles, Russell Hudson, Patrick McCarthy, Patrick Hodges, Sam F.S. Chin, Kwan Sai-Hung, Martin Pickands, Bruce Juchnik, and Zhuang Jiaren.

Pai-Lum, Pai-Shou, and White Lotus training manuals, policy documents, letters, handouts, and notes. The most important being:
1. Pai Lum Association: Policy Document 1980-001
2. Organization of the Pai Shou Athletic Association, April 1981

Articles from the following publications:
Black belt magazine: 1960 – 1989
Karate Outlook Magazine: 1974
Martial Arts of China: 1990 – 1991
Inside Kung Fu: 1981 – 2000
Secrets of Kung Fu: 1974 – 1977
Internal Arts Magazine: 1989 – 1991
Professional Karate: 1974
Karate (Karate/Kung Fu) Illustrated: 1970 – 1989
YMAA newsletter: 1987 – 1989
Pa-Kua Journal: 1990 -1997
International Ryukyu Karate Research Society: 2009 to present.

Of the above publications, articles, monthly columns, and letters from the following authors may have been used as reference material:
Adam Hsu, Yang Jwing Ming, Patrick McCarthy, John P. Painter, Doc Fai Wong, John S. Wang, Dan Miller, Tim Cartmell, Jane Hallander, Daniel Weng, Scott Wong, Steve Martin, Kwong Wing Lam, Liang Shou Yu, George Xu, Daniel Farber, Kenneth S. Cohen, Frank De-Maria, Peter Chema, Al Dacascos, Paul Okami, Yang Yashan and Eric Sbarge.

SECOND GENERATION STUDENT LIST

This portion of the Pai Family lineage is an alphabetic listing of second-generation students, practitioners, instructors, disciples, and adopted Grandchildren of the first-generation founder of the Pai Family Arts, Daniel K. Pai. It is not laid out in a specific "Rank" or "Seniority" oriented manner.

People on this list were issued certificates of rank or similar documents for 1st higher level/1st-degree black belt or above that are signed by Grandmaster Daniel K. Pai. Included are people who have attained first higher level through training, were given honorary first higher level status, or their rank in previous training was recognized by the late Grandmaster, Daniel K. Pai.

Being on this list does not automatically imply or verify that an individual is certified to teach Pai-Lum or is a Senior Student, Disciple, or adopted Grandchild of Daniel K. Pai. Those positions are covered by additional documentation.

There are three categories of rank or grade certificates that have Daniel K. Pai's signature:

1. Certificates or similar documents issued by Daniel K. Pai or training halls he operated before the Pai-Lum Association was created. Such as the Richmond Judo and Karate Club, Pai Defensive Arts Studio, and Pai Karate Institute.

2. Certificates or similar documents issued through the Pai-Lum Association, Fire Dragon Incorporated, Bok Leen Pai Temple, US White Dragon Martial Arts Society, World White Dragon Kung-Fu Society, or other Pai-Lum governing body between 1972 and May 28, 1993.

3. Certificates not issued through a Pai-Lum governing body between 1963 and May 28, 1993. This type of certificate usually recognizes some level of competence in the art(s) taught by the issuing body; it does not entitle the holder to claim rank in the Pai Family arts.

Certificates of attendance or participation in training seminars signed by Daniel K. Pai do not denote rank or level of achievement.

Everyone on this list has attained or was given, an honorary 1st Higher Level or above, with a certificate signed by Daniel K. Pai.

The following keys will follow some of the names on this list:

*   First person promoted to 4th higher level (May 1972) by Daniel K. Pai.

**   The original four people to serve on the Council of Grandchildren.

***   The original two people with adopted Granddaughter status.

**** People with status in more than one generation, i.e., 2nd and 3rd generation. In this case, when a student of a second-generation instructor is also accepted as a student by Daniel K. Pai.

\+   Primary training is not Pai-Lum.
These people knew, associated, and trained with Daniel K. Pai; they may or may not have been adopted as "Disciples" or "Grandchildren."

(D)   Deceased.

William Luciano created this list as a general reference guide using available information. No disrespect is meant for anyone who is left out or listed in the wrong category. This list was created on 10/27/1996 and was revised in May 2025.

1st Generation-Founder

DANIEL KANE PAI
(Daniel Kalima'ahaae Pa'i)
1930 - 1993
Pai T'ien-Lung [Bai Tianlong 白天龍]
Pai Tan-Ni [Bai Danni 白丹尼

2nd Generation-students

STEVEN ALSUP (D) +

ERIC BANNON

MARY SHAWN BAYER
(Pai Mei-Ling)

JANET BEER

WILLIAM BITTORF

HENRY G. BOWERS (D)

RAY CARPENTER

TONY CARPANZANO

CHRIS CASEY (D) +
 (Pai Chi-Lum)

TERRY CERMOLA
(Pai Ren-Ai)

SUZY CHAPPEL

GEORGE CHARTIER (D) +

DAPHNE COLLINS

LARRY COLLINS (D)

DON COLLYER (D) +

CLARENCE COOPER

WARREN COTTRELL

MIKE CRAIN +
(resigned)

JIM CRAVENS +
(resigned)

GINO CRETELLA (D) + ****

BRUCE CURRIE +

RICK DEAN +

DENIS DECKER (D) +
(Pai Tao-Chung)

JOE DEUSHLE

SHAWN DICK (D)
(Pai Xue-Long)

GEORGE DILLMAN +

MIKE DOUCET + ****
(Pai T'ieh-Lung)

ROBERT DUTCHER
(Pai Tai Ki Su)

ROY EIDEM (D)

DAVID EVERETT **
(Pai Tao-Ch'i)
(resigned)

CHARLES FISHER (D) +

KRIS FRISSORA

TONY GALIANO

RICH GALICIA ****

PETER GIARNIERO ****

Appendix F

ADRIAN GOMES (D) +

JOHN GUERRERA

CAROL GUIFFRE

JEFF GUIFFRE (D)
(Pai Quan-Li)

BETH GUISER

BILL GREGORY (D) +
(Pai Meng-Hu)

KALAII KANO GRIFFIN (D) +

THERESA FRUEND
(Pai Lieh-Lang)

CHARLES HATCHETT (D) ****

CHEYENNE HASUSER

LIONEL HARMON

BUDDY HEGE +

RICK HODISH

DON HOWARD (D)
(Pai Yong-Lee)

RUSTY HUDSON
(Pai Hsiung-Chi)

PHIL HUNTER (D)
(Pai Hsin-Lung)

CYNTHIA HUTTON
(Pai Yu-Lung)

DAVID JACOBS

DAN KARGER
(Pai Ban-Lung)

CHRIS KASUTA
(Pai T'iao Mao Lung)

MIKE KAYLOR (D)
(Bai Mai-Long)

JACK LANNOM +

ANN LAYROCK BORIS
(Pai Lo-Long)

PAULETTE LEVY

CHOW LUM

RON LYDESTAD (D) **+
(Pai Li-Chung)
(Lee C. Pai)

RICH MACEY

STEVE MATHEWS ****
(Pai Shao-Li)

PATRICK McCARTHY +

BRUCE McKNIGHT
(Bai Shi Long)

LAWRENCE McSWAIN (D) +

DANIEL MILLER

DARRYL E. MIZER +

DANA MONTE

SHERI MORTIMER
(Pai Tzu-Lan)

AL MUELLER

JAMES MUSIC ****

CONNIE NORRIS

THOMAS O'BRIANT

PAUL OLSON (D) +

MARCIA PICKANDS (D) ***
(Pai Pai-He)

MARTIN PICKANDS

LAUREN PORTER
(Pai Lung-Nu)

CHARLES POWELL +
(Pai Bac-Kua)

JEFF (KUMAR) RATHNUM

KEN REGENNITTER (D) +
(Pai Jen-Ching)

JOHN RIDDICK ****
(Pai Lin-Lung)

DON RIDDLE (D) +

LAURIE GOMON RING

STEVE ROSENZWEIG (D)
(Pai An-Lung)

JAMES ROE

THOMAS D. ST. CHARLES (D) *
(Pai Shin-Zan)

THOMAS SANDERS ****

FRED SCHMITZ (D)
(Pai Sen-Chuan)

BOB SCHOOLNICK (D) +

ISRAEL (YOGI) SEGARRA (D) +

HONEY SILK
(Pai Lung-Li)

ROBERT L. SKALING (D) +
(Pai Ying-Lung)
(Robert Skaling-Pai)

DAVID L. SMITH (D) **
(Pai Tso-Ching /Pai Ching-Lin)

BILL SNOUFFER (D) ****

JOAN SPIEDEL
(Pai Fen-Mien)

KAREN SQUILLANTE
(Pai Ping-Lung)

ED STROK + ****
(Pai Zhi-Lung)

KEN TALLACK +

GENE THORNER (D) +
(Pai Kua-Po)

KAREN TOLCZYK
(Hun Gai Lung Po Pai)

TOM TURCOTTE +

RICH VENIZIANO

DENISE VIGI (D)

PHILIP VIMINI

VITO VINCENZO

TED VOLRATH (D) +

GLENN WANDY

JANICE WENINGER ***
(Pai Kwan-Li / Pai She-Wang)

JOHN A. WENINGER (D) **
(Pai Li-Lung)

DON WILSON +

GLENN WILSON +

JIM WILSON

STAN WILSON

GEORGE YOUNKER

THE MARTIAL LINEAGE
OF THE
PAI-FAMILY MARTIAL TRAINING ASSOCIATION

PAI-CHIA CH'ÜAN
(PAI-LUM)

PAI-LIN CH'ÜAN

SHAOLIN SHIH-PA T'ENG-JEN FA

This lineage covers primarily the arts of Grandmaster Daniel K. Pai and Grandmaster Ch'en Chin-Yuan.

The Daniel K. Pai (Pai Family Martial Arts) lineage lists the senior Students/ Disciples of David L. Smith (Pai Ching-Lin), Marcia L. Pickands (Pai Pai-He), and two of John Weninger's (Pai Li-Lung) senior Students who also trained with David L. Smith in the South Shaolin Eighteen Bronze-Man Method

The Ch'en Chin-Yuan (South Shaolin Eighteen Bronze-Man Method) lineage lists the senior Students/Disciples of David L. Smith.

In addition, there are other teachers that Mr. Smith has trained under and has passed along elements of their teachings.

Ralph Lindquist
Isshin-Ryu

Louis Casamassa
Okinawan Kempo

Hsieh Hsin-Keng
謝辛庚
T'ien Shan P'ai
T'ung-I T'ang

Wang Tsao-Yang
王昭陽
Southern
Luohan Fist

Ma Tsao-Jih
馬朝日
Feeding Crane
Golden Eagle

Lin I-Shen
林益生
Fukien
Yung Ch'un Ch'

David L. Smith
白靜林
Pai Ching-Lin

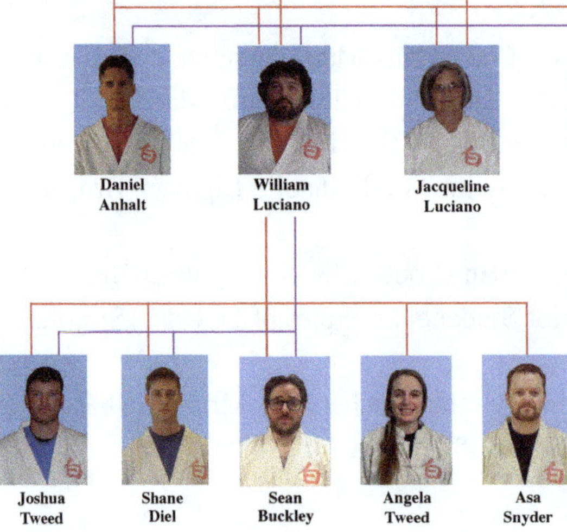

**Daniel
Anhalt**

**William
Luciano**

**Jacqueline
Luciano**

**Anne
Sutton**

**J.E.
Neeland**

**Joshua
Tweed**

**Shane
Diel**

**Sean
Buckley**

**Angela
Tweed**

**Asa
Snyder**

SOUTH SHAOLIN
18 BRONZEMAN METHOD

金源武德會

u Keng-Hsin
周庚辛
Shaolin
Ch'in-Na

Daniel K. Pai
白天龍
Grandmaster
Pai Family Martial Arts
(Pai-Lum Kung-Fu)

Ch'en Chin-Yuan
陳金源
Grandmaster
South Shaolin Eighteen
Bronze Man Method

Marcia Pickands
白白鶴
Pai Pai-He

John Weninger
白立龍
Pai Li-Lung

orman
ohnson

Vincent
Antonelli

Andrew
St.John

Ed
Walters

Michael
Rothermel

Millie
Ramos-Rothermel

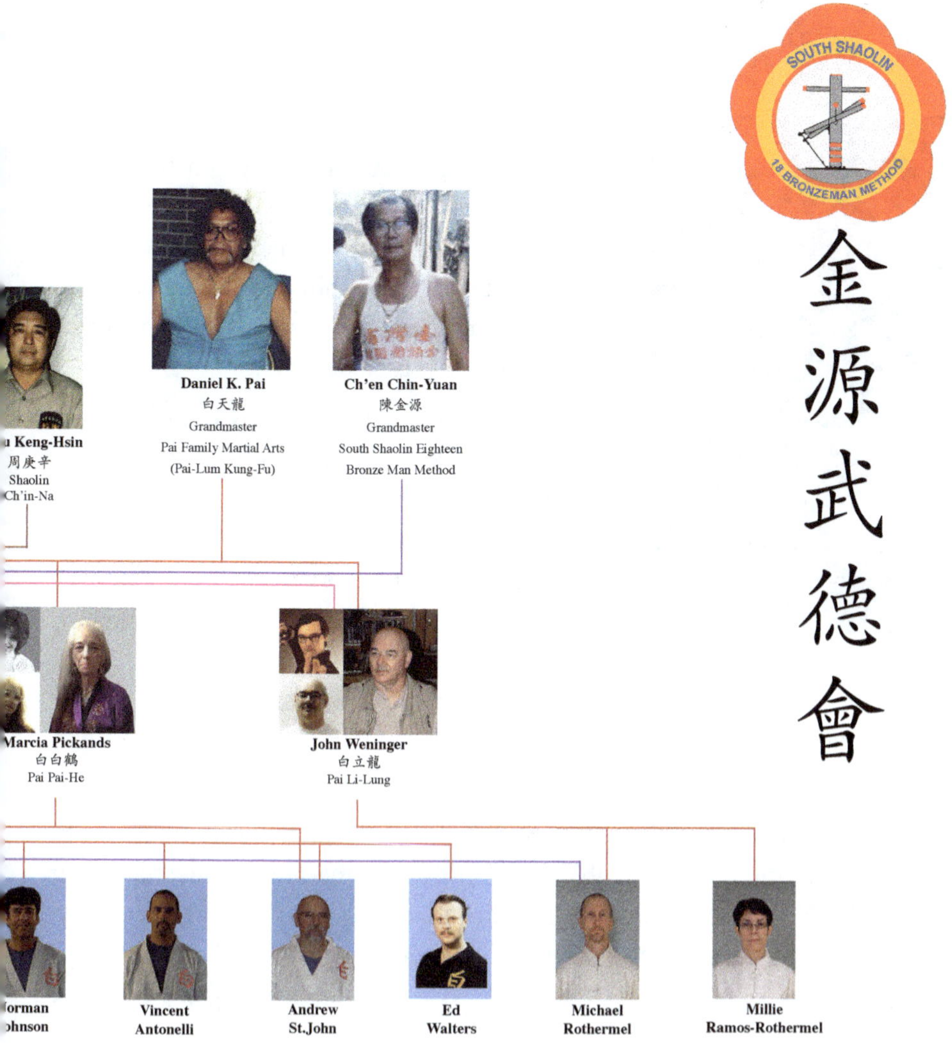

Appendix G

About the Author

WILLIAM LUCIANO

William Luciano is a life-long practitioner of martial arts. He began training Pai-Lum Kung-Fu at age 12 from 1973 to 1976, had a five-year break in training, and began again in 1981; he has been involved ever since. He has been independently teaching martial arts since 1987.

In all, William had three primary teachers in the art of Pai-Lum: Richard Macey (1973-1976), Marcia L. Pickands (1981-1987), and David L. Smith (1987-2023); additional training in Pai-Lum was with the following teachers (listed in order of influence): Grandmaster Daniel K. Pai, Thomas D. St. Charles, Phil Hunter, John Weninger, Steve Mathews, and Daniel Anhalt while concurrently training in the arts of the South Shaolin Eighteen Bronze Man Method, Southern Luo-Han Method, and T'ung-I T'ang Kuo-Shu under David L. Smith.

William also has experience in a variety of martial arts, having trained with or influenced by a large number of practitioners, the most influential being Steven Nacua, Patrick Hodges, Sam Chin, Kwan Sai-Hung, Patrick McCarthy, Yang Jwing-Ming, Liang Shou-Yu, Bruce Juchnik, and Vince Ward.

William currently teaches Pai-Chia Ch'üan (Pai-Lum/Pai-Lin Ch'üan) and the South Shaolin Eighteen Bronze Man Method at his private training hall (Ying-Hao Wu-Kung Kuan) in Upstate, NY.

www.ingramcontent.com/pod-product-compliance
Lightning Source LLC
Chambersburg PA
CBHW071639030726
47592CB00008B/2860